Empire of the Mind

A Journey Through Great Britain

I Q B A L   A H M E D

COLDSTREAM PUBLISHERS

First Published in Great Britain in 2006 by
COLDSTREAM PUBLISHERS
27 Savernake Road
London NW3 2JT
coldstreampublishers@hotmail.com

Copyright © Iqbal Ahmed, 2006

Designed and produced in Great Britain by
Clinton Smith Design

A CIP catalogue record for this book is available from the British Library.

ISBN 0-9548080-1-0

My sincere gratitude to the

ARTS COUNCIL ENGLAND

for their invaluable support.

And now I would wake up, troubled and inexact,
from that shallow sleep in which dreams precede sunrise,
as the vague mind cautiously acknowledges the fact

Derek Walcott: *Omeros*

Contents

Oxford Blue

I heard the word 'Oxbridge' so often in London that for some time I considered Oxford and Cambridge to be twin cities in a single county. In my mistaken belief, I resembled someone who has confused this portmanteau name with the small town of 'Uxbridge' in Middlesex. Robert the Concierge, who had been to Srinagar many years ago, told me one day that he had met a certain houseboat owner there who spoke to him with 'an educated Oxford accent'. It was a revelation to me that education and a mode of pronunciation were linked together as one in this part of the world. I had neither money nor inclination to visit Oxford or Cambridge during my first few years in London. A middle-aged husband and wife, who both by some strange coincidence had red hair, told me once in Hampstead that, being students, they travelled every week from London to Oxford. Their use of the word 'students' seemed ostentatious to me.

My first acquaintance with Oxford was an English dictionary published by the Oxford University Press in New Delhi. I had persuaded my uncle to part with seventy-five rupees for me to buy a copy from a bookshop in Srinagar. It was a large amount, nearly five times the price one paid for a textbook, or enough money to pay fees for a term in a private school. It had therefore taken me several months to convince my uncle that I really needed an English dictionary. When I asked the bookseller for a receipt to show to my uncle, he refused to write one, thinking that I might want to return it the next day and ask for a refund. He warned me that a dictionary once sold could not be returned.

I found it difficult in the beginning to use an English-to-English dictionary as I had to look up many words in order to find the meaning of an unfamiliar one. I didn't mind this perpetual searching because it made me familiar with new words. A poet has rightly compared the Oxford Dictionary to an empire.

Fourteen years after acquiring my first dictionary, I moved to London without it. A few months later, I bought a new one from an academic bookshop in Charing Cross Road. My Concise Oxford Dictionary had gained twenty thousand words and I was surprised to find that the price of a fat dictionary was less than a slim textbook.

I arrived at Marylebone Station one morning, hoping to catch a train to Oxford. The man behind the counter, who wore a blue turban, said that I could travel to Banbury from there but not to Oxford, and I must go to Paddington to catch the right train. I liked Marylebone Station, which is hidden behind a Gothic Revival-style building. It is a small Victorian station with a wrought-iron canopy connecting it to an elegant building that functions as a luxury hotel. I had to cycle along a busy road to reach Paddington Station, in close proximity to which I discovered virtually a new town being built in glass and iron. An iron bridge near the station was closed for traffic so I had to follow a diversion that took me a mile and a half past the station.

I had to cycle back to Paddington by another route to catch my train. It pulled out of the station past these new buildings. Through the window of a slow-moving coach, the large number of tower blocks in West London became very apparent. The bold colours of graffiti on the brick walls along the railway tracks were blackened by the elements. The train passed through an industrial landscape until it reached Slough. A few disused warehouses along the railway track had been turned into self-storage facilities with yard-high letters on their exterior walls glaring at commuters. The names of factories like ICI and Horlicks reminded me of their commercials, broadcast on *Delhi Doordarshan* during my childhood. A tall, slim chimney arising from the chocolate-drink factory was covered with resinous soot.

The landscape transformed into green fields beyond Slough and then became undulating, with a few chalk hills in sight along the route. Halfway between London and Oxford, the train stopped at Reading and a few smartly dressed men and women got off. Reading has modern office buildings occupied by businesses which specialize in information technology. These office buildings are surrounded by vast car parks, giving it the feel of a commuter town. I could see at a distance the high columns of the power station at Didcot billowing smoke into the sky. Many passengers were getting ready to alight at Oxford.

I had expected it to be a Victorian station but it turned out to be more contemporary. One or two large posters announced an evangelical event in London. I tried to hail a taxi outside the station to Cornmarket Street where I was to meet Hashim in a few minutes. The taxi-driver dissuaded me by saying that it was only a short walk away from the station. Across the road, a newly constructed building with a multi-tiered tower which looked like a pagoda rising above it had 'University of Oxford' engraved above its entrance. It housed 'The Said Business School'. I walked hurriedly past the building towards the town centre. Oxford seemed very serene compared to London. Its stone buildings looked mellow in the afternoon sun.

Hashim was waiting for me at the coffee-shop in Cornmarket when I arrived. I had met him in London a few times in the last two years. He was in his early twenties and came from a wealthy family in the Sultanate of Oman. Married for three years, his wife had dutifully accompanied him to Oxford. They lived in a rented house in Abingdon just outside the town. Hashim owned an expensive car which he mostly used for travelling to London at weekends, preferring to commute by taxi from Abingdon to Oxford. He received a monthly allowance of four thousand pounds from his father. He spent a quarter of it on the rent of his house and another quarter towards his college fees. The rest of it covered his weekend expenses in London. He had recently asked his father to increase his allowance to five thousand pounds a month. His father had a big family. Hashim was the youngest of fourteen children and his eldest brother was twenty-four years older than him.

It had always been his father's ambition to send one of his sons to Oxford. In fact, Hashim attended a private college there. He was quite frank about it. He told me that it was beyond him to gain admission to one of the colleges which constituted the University of Oxford and his father was happy enough to see him enrolled as a student in an Oxford private college. He had sent another son to a business school in America. Hashim's brothers often visited London, staying in a hotel in Park Lane. Their father owned a big flat near Marble Arch but they preferred to stay in a hotel. The flat had been empty for the last ten years. I had also met one of Hashim's brothers in London. He was a car enthusiast and liked to drive a different sports car every other day. Unlike his brother, Hashim was an unassuming person.

The coffee-shop was full of schoolchildren and therefore very noisy. I wished I had arranged to meet Hashim elsewhere. He was going to finish his business course in a few months time and looked forward to going home. I asked him about the business school I had seen opposite the train station. He told me that it was built with the financial help of a Middle Eastern businessman called Said and the college was given the name of its benefactor. I had assumed that it was dedicated to a scholar of the same name. The funding of the Said Business School had caused controversy and the Oxford Union wanted students to boycott the school as a venue for various activities.

Hashim's college enrolled mostly foreign students and he had become friends with Hitaki from Nagasaki. Hashim had travelled to Japan with his wife a few months earlier to visit Hitaki's family. I asked him if he had made any friends among the people of Oxfordshire. He said that there were only two he'd got to know during the last two years: his tutor and the woman who came to clean his house twice a week. He considered himself lucky to have his wife accompany him to Oxford. He escaped to London during the weekends to meet other members of his family who visited the town often. It made his life in Oxford bearable.

Cornmarket Street was a pedestrian thoroughfare, full of shoppers in the afternoon. It offered me the familiar sight of a high street in London, with young women wearing white sweatshirts and gold necklaces and pushing baby buggies. One could also see elderly women pulling their shopping bags on wheels. And a large group of visiting Italian schoolchildren was walking down the street with their teachers. Cornmarket Street had fast food restaurants like

Burger King and McDonald's. It also had the usual shops selling mobile phones and video games. Only the benches made of steel and basalt along the street were of unusual shape.

Hashim wanted to show me Magdalen Bridge, famous for the May-day celebrations. From Cornmarket Street, we turned into High Street, which has more colleges and fewer shops. Hashim could not identify the individual colleges for me and only remembered the name of Magdalen College because it was located near Magdalen Bridge. Like certain other discreet establishments, these colleges withheld their names. Walking down High Street and catching a glimpse of a cloister through a narrow gate, it occurred to me that until the beginning of the twentieth century all the learning in this town was religious. Each college was built around a chapel and attendance at a service on Sunday was compulsory.

A few punts sat idle near the bridge. Children in uniform were pouring out of a school on the other side of the bridge. Hashim mentioned that High Street becomes Cowley Road after a roundabout. I remember Robert the Concierge divulging to me in London a few weeks earlier that Oxford becomes rough after the roundabout known as The Plain. I asked Hashim to accompany me on a walk along Cowley Road.

It had many groceries run by Asians. It also had a number of Indian restaurants and ramshackle accommodation for poorer students. I was surprised to see a

Russian delicatessen among the shops selling ethnic gear. The images of Cowley Road displayed in the Museum of Oxford tried to paint a picture of diversity. For the last four years, Cowley Road had held a summer carnival that, according to its organizers, helped the people of Oxford to mix a bit. It was an ambitious project. Walking in this part of the town, I felt as if I had been transported from the academic world on the other side of Magdalen Bridge into a nether world where people were engaged mainly in manual work. However, quite a few students seemed to be relaxing in bars and restaurants in Cowley Road. Hashim told me that he came here often to eat in a North African restaurant.

It was getting dark by the time we crossed Magdalen Bridge again on our way back. The bus stop was crowded and a tearoom nearby was filled with students. Some students were riding their bicycles in the narrow side-roads. Others were riding on the pavement. I had seen a tangle of bicycles outside the train station; there were also bicycles leaning against the walls outside the college gates. One could not leave a bicycle like this in London without chaining it to a fence or a lamppost. Hashim explained why he preferred to take a taxi rather than drive his own car in Oxford. The roads were narrow and the traffic moved mostly in one direction. He also told me that it was obligatory for an Oxford undergraduate to live within six miles of the tower known as Carfax .

We came back to the coffee-shop in Cornmarket Street. It was less crowded now, most of the shoppers having already gone home. Hashim was waiting for his friend, Hitaki, to join us. He had gone to Bicester Village for the day and arrived in due course with two or three stylish shopping bags. Since Bicester has mostly designer outlets. I hadn't expected a student to go there for shopping. Hitaki had bought a pair of shoes and new glasses. He tried on his new glasses to show them to Hashim. They made him look more like an intellectual. When I asked Hitaki how much he had spent on his shopping that day, he replied that it was just over two hundred pounds. These were discount outlets, he explained; the normal price for his purchases would have been five hundred pounds. Hitaki seemed happy with his bargains. He said that he went to Bicester once a month. He worked in a bar in George Street in the evenings and his wages were just enough for his monthly shopping trip. His other expenses were being taken care of by his parents. He would also buy gifts for them. They liked British brands like Burberry.

Hashim invited us to join him for dinner at his home. Hitaki and I chose to take a bus to Abingdon instead of a taxi. Two American students were sitting in front of us. I overheard one of them saying that she had been to Abingdon in Virginia, America. Oxford is a popular destination for Americans; one frequently hears American accents echoing in the narrow lanes of the town. I had passed an American bar and grill restaurant near the train station. Another American theme restaurant further up the road served steak and ribs and was frequented by students from different countries. Oxford inspires awe in Americans. They have seen images of the town in many films. The University ranked behind American universities in a recent educational poll; but the town still casts a spell on many Americans. Even the philosopher and poet, Ralph Waldo Emerson, was overwhelmed by Oxford. Americans raise funds in their country to finance many projects at the University.

We got off the bus at Abingdon. Hashim lived in a house near the County Hall. It was Rose the cleaning lady who opened the door for us. She cleaned the house for Hashim and his wife twice a week and sometimes came round in the evening to have a meal with them. The living-room was crammed with furniture that belonged to the landlord. Hashim's wife, Zubeidah, was preparing food in the kitchen. She came into the living-room to greet her guests, her head covered in a black scarf. Rose laid a table in the dining-room. As they did not speak a common language, Zubeidah and Rose understood each other by gestures alone. Hashim said that his wife never cooked any food at their family home in Muscat. In fact, she had only learnt to cook when they moved to Oxford two years ago. They had found it tedious to eat out every night. Besides, Abingdon didn't have a wide variety of restaurants. Hashim liked to eat out in London, frequenting different restaurants in Edgware Road.

I asked him why he liked Edgware Road restaurants particularly. It was because of a certain type of bread they served with food there, he said, very similar to the bread they ate at home in Muscat. He also liked the relaxed atmosphere of the restaurants around Marble Arch where people smoked oriental-style pipes.

I asked Hashim how his wife filled her day in Abingdon. He said that she looked forward to her weekends in London where she usually met other members of their big family. The women in the family stayed together while the men engaged in their own conversations. Hashim wanted to start a family. They had been trying to have a baby for some time and had been to see a doctor in Harley Street in London a few times.

A few weeks later, I travelled to Oxford again, this time for a walking tour. The starting point of the tour was in Broad Street, where I found a group of people gathered around a guide. He was an Oxfordshire man with a dry sense of humour. He spoke with a drawl like a university professor. Broad Street got its name, he said, from being broader than other streets in Oxford. He proceeded to relate the history of the University, telling us how many British Prime Ministers had been educated in its colleges. I had assumed that the people of Oxfordshire had a disregard for power until I heard this long list of names. I suddenly remembered that half of the British Viceroys who ruled India were educated at

Oxford, including Lord Curzon, who had composed a verse during his time there:

> 'My name is George Nathaniel Curzon
> I am a most superior person.'

His name became proverbial in the Indian subcontinent for a high-minded person. Oxford University has also produced Cecil Rhodes – a twentieth-century imperialist. In the second half of the last century, both freedom fighters and nationalists in the former colonies have sent their children to Oxford to study History and Economics. The guide mentioned the names of the colleges where Mrs Gandhi and Mrs Bhutto – the two most fearsome Prime Ministers of the subcontinent – were educated.

Our first port of call was Jesus College. We followed the guide into the quad where the grass was as velvety as a bowling green. He led us into a corner for a commentary. He kept his voice low but it echoed inside the quad. One could imagine the monastic life of students during earlier days, when the students wore black gowns out of clerical habit. The guide stopped outside the gates of Trinity for an introductory lecture on notable former pupils of the college. The first name he mentioned was Richard Burton – not the actor but the nineteenth century explorer. He was rusticated after only a brief stay. He felt he had 'fallen among grocers' in Oxford. Burton joined the East India Company as a lieutenant, translated the *Kama Sutra* and *The Arabian Nights* into English and, it is said, learnt to speak Arabic like a native. Edward

Gibbon – another Oxford man – had read the *Arabian Nights* a century before Burton's translation and then produced an epic book, *The Decline and Fall of the Roman Empire*, claiming that his writing owed no obligation to Oxford.

We followed the guide to the other end of Broad Street, where we found the circular Sheldonian Theatre building, guarded by a row of statues of bearded men mounted on high pedestals. The Sheldonian Theatre is not a playhouse but a venue for University public ceremonies. The building was designed by Christopher Wren, who based it on Serlio's illustration of the Theatre of Marcellus. Wren also designed the garden quadrangle of Trinity College. It was in a room within the roof structure of the Sheldonian Theatre that Oxford University Press began its existence.

The next building we saw was Radcliffe Camera. Its name suggested that it was an observatory. The building had a dome with circular windows but there was no telescope available to observe the heavenly bodies. Radcliffe Camera was used as a reading room. It was designed by James Gibbs, based on the plan of Hawksmoor – an apprentice of Christopher Wren. The guide apologized that the reading room was not open to the public. In fact, Radcliffe Camera is a part of the Bodleian Library. The library's exhibition room was open to the public, but I had no wish to see it as I preferred the British Library to the Bodleian, which in any case I'd visited before.

The tour finished in Cattle Street. There on view was a group of young men in tweed jackets and caps holding placards denouncing the ban on fox hunting. They were seeking support for the Countryside Alliance among the students. It was bizarre to see such young people clad in the gear of the elderly. Before the guide bade us farewell, I asked him what colour exactly was Oxford blue. He pointed out a dark shade of blue to me and stated that light blue is the hideous Cambridge preference. I was surprised by his strength of feeling.

I had been intrigued by the words *Dominus illuminate mea*, which appear in a book on the University coat of arms. Then one day I chanced upon these Latin words, meaning 'The Lord is my life', in Psalms. It reminded me that the University's origins were sacred rather than secular. Discouraging the teaching of Sciences for many years, the University instructed its pupils in Theology, Rhetoric and Christian Doctrine so that they could serve the church after leaving. Oxford has given birth to the Christian denomination known as Methodism. Its founder, Charles Wesley, was an Oxford man, who stated: 'My first year in college I lost in diversion; the next I set myself to study. Diligence led me into serious thinking; I went to the weekly Sacrament, persuaded two or three young students to accompany me and to observe the methods of study prescribed by the university. This gained me the harmless name *Methodist*.' It was in 1729 that his brother John Wesley joined the fellowship and became its leader.

Although Oxford is a centre of book publishing in the UK, and the industry contributes to the economy of the town by employing many people, it is difficult to describe it as a literary place. The town is mostly associated with a few children's writers. While browsing in one of its bookshops, I enquired about an obscure title by Marcel Proust. The bookseller misheard the name of the author as Provost. I gave up my search for the book and left the shop. The first book printed in Oxford appeared in 1478 AD – a year after Caxton printed the first book in England. But the most important development came two centuries later, when Oxford University Press was founded. It was to become the largest employer in Victorian Oxford.

It had gone dark and the autumn evening felt chilly. I had spent only half a day in Oxford. I was undecided whether to spend the night there or take a train back to London. But the prospect of spending a night in the town was daunting; the limited choice of accommodation persuaded me to return to London.

When I met Hashim again in London two months later, he asked me to join him and his family for an end-of-term feast in Oxford. He had invited his brothers and their families, as well as Hitaki and his tutor, Mr Anderson. Hashim was hosting the banquet in the dining hall of an Oxford hotel. I accepted his invitation gladly because

I wanted to visit the town again.

I arrived an hour before the banquet to saunter along the streets and drifted towards the north side of the town where I discovered a neoclassical building: the Ashmolean Museum in Beamont Street. The collection of the museum was donated to the university by Elias Ashmole, the son of a saddler and an alchemist by profession. I didn't have much time to explore the museum. I walked to the end of Beaumont Street – a newspaper vendor had corrected my pronunciation of this street name earlier – and then turned right to discover Walton Street signposted, the name of the road which appeared as the address of Oxford University Press inside my Concise Dictionary.

The Concise Oxford Dictionary has never ceased to surprise me. Many times, I have believed certain words to mean the opposite of their actual meaning, so often, in fact, that I wonder at my own folly. It has taken me a number of years to find my way through the quarter of a million words in the Concise Dictionary, which has taught me bizarre inflections of familiar words. I am also fascinated by the thinness of its paper and its whiteness, which hasn't yellowed even after many years of ownership. One day a water-colour artist told me that this is because the Dictionary is printed on acid-free paper. Only my dictionary has proved to be a reliably present tutor for me in the realm of literature. Our milkman in Srinagar called a lexicon a 'diction-war'.

The OUP has its headquarter in Walton Street in an

impressively grand-looking building. It is actually a department of the University of Oxford, which obtained a decree from the Star Chamber in the seventeenth century confirming its privilege to print books. The University also established its right to print the King James Authorized Version of the Bible and this additional privilege formed the basis of a lucrative business throughout the next two centuries. The OUP opened its first overseas office in America in 1896, followed by offices in many colonial cities around the world. It has its own bookshop in High Street in Oxford. I had been there on one of my earlier visits but it was so full of academic titles that I did not venture beyond its reference books section.

I found the home of the Oxford Union in St Michael's Street. It looked like a miniature House of Commons from the inside and it is indeed where many future Members of Parliament in Britain learn their debating skills. The topic to be debated later that day was 'whether mass media undermines democracy'. Among the participants was a BBC journalist who was deemed to have undermined the Corporation itself a few months earlier. The original debating hall had been turned into the library of the debating society; its walls decorated with murals by William Morris and Burne-Jones. I had caught a glimpse of their famous tapestry, *The Adoration of the Magi*, in the chapel of Exeter College.

I found a synagogue at the north end of Oxford – an unusual sight in a church town. There are a few Jewish families living in the city. The Jewish settlement began with Oliver Cromwell, who had dealings with Jewish people to acquire funds and permitted them to return to England after a period of banishment. Oxford University initially encouraged them to convert to Christianity. At the end of the eighteenth century, people of Jewish descent began to figure in the University in increasing numbers, but it was not until the second half of the nineteenth century that they were admitted as members of the University.

I reached the hotel where Hashim was hosting the banquet for his family and friends just in time. His brothers had already arrived with their wives and children, accompanied by two nannies, one of whom had grown up in their house in Muscat. Hashim's tutor, Mr Anderson, arrived shortly after and Hitaki was the last one to join the party. Mr Anderson was in his late fifties, a well-travelled rather eccentric man, who played the role of chief guest at the banquet. He had a profound understanding of other cultures and had picked up Arabic while teaching English in a Middle Eastern country. However, he said that being an Englishman gave him no incentive whatsoever to learn other languages. Hashim's older brother was delighted to hear him speaking Arabic. Mr Anderson knew the history of the Sultanate of Oman very well, mentioning the name of the British political agent who advised the Sultan in Muscat in the 1960s. Hashim's brother was happy to seek his advice in a business matter. Mr Anderson wanted him to donate some money to a charity in Oxford, since he knew Hashim's family supported several such good causes. Hashim's brother gave Mr Anderson a few hundred pounds for Oxfam, which was founded here in 1942 as the Oxford Committee for Famine Relief.

The college tutors in Oxford were known for their silence while dining with their pupils. But Mr Anderson was a very lively person, entertaining everyone with his conversation and easy manner. When Hashim's brother invited him to their family home in Muscat, he accepted. Mr Anderson liked the idea of travelling. He had been to more than sixty countries yet continued to live in a rented property in Oxford. His current landlord was an Asian shopkeeper. He remembered the time when Asians arrived in Oxford for the first time. They were employed by a private bus company called City of Oxford Motor Services, which had failed to attract local men because they had moved to better-paid jobs offered by Morris Motors.

The train station was quiet at nine in the evening, with just a few people waiting on the platform for the next train to London. I recognized Dr Aggarwal sitting on a bench, a man whom I saw now and again in a shop in Hampstead. Dr Aggarwal had qualified as a doctor in Maharashtra in India before settling in Britain. He was surprised to see me in Oxford. He had come to see his daughter and was extremely proud that she had been accepted as a student by an Oxford college. He told me that she was very diligent and that it would be easier for his grandchildren to gain admission to a college in Oxford now that his daughter was a student there. I was taken aback by the extent of Dr Aggarwal's ambition.

Before my first journey to Oxford, I had asked my friend Robert the Concierge what he thought of the town. He said that it was like Hampstead in London. This seemed a bizarre comparison to me. I had heard a few people in Hampstead occasionally uttering a Latin phrase and assumed that they had been to Oxford. I had for some time even toyed with the idea of leaving London and living in Oxford. But the idea seemed absurd to me after I started travelling outside London. I would have been lost without the places I haunted in London. It gave me a sense of profound well-being to be back in London that evening.

Auntie's Teashop in Cambridge

On my first visit to Cambridge a few years ago, I took my bicycle with me on the train and then found it irksome to ride it there. In Cambridge there are more cyclists on the road than in London. I was not used to having so many fellow-cyclists trailing me along a narrow route. So I chained my bicycle to a stand near the train station and walked instead. On my second visit to Cambridge, I decided to board a train at King's Cross without my bicycle.

The regeneration of King's Cross that was taking shape could be seen from afar. The flat concrete structure of the new Eurostar terminal had risen behind the catacombs of the old station. The Gothic building near the station was being refurbished to be used as a hotel again. I had often wondered why this building overlooking the British Library had fallen into disuse. But I rarely crossed Midland Road, which separated the library from St Pancras Station.

At first I was disconcerted by the new location of the British Library at King's Cross. When I visited it a few months after it was officially opened by the Queen I was informed at the membership desk that it was a national library and therefore open only to scholarly members of the public. My request for a reader's ticket was denied. A year later, while stopping at a bicycle shop in Camden Town, I noticed that the person repairing my bike was carrying a British Library membership card in his shirt pocket. It gave me courage to try again. I wanted to browse the catalogue of the India Office Records in one of its reading rooms. These records are the documentary archive of the administration in London of the British government in India. This time, the woman at the membership desk found my request for a reader's card convincing and issued me with one. Since then I have spent more time in its Humanities reading room than the India Office Records section. I became fonder of the new British Library. At first, I had reservations about its English Free School style of architecture but I eventually became oblivious of the exterior of the building and its nearness to King's Cross.

I had arranged to meet Tao Yang at the main entrance of King's Cross Station to catch a train to Cambridge. Tao was a Cambridge student who spent her summer holidays in London, working in a coffee-shop. I got to know her during the period of her summer job. Her name reminded me of the Tao Café in Srinagar, a charming name for a café housed in a cottage shaded by giant plane trees. This café was a retreat for a few troubled souls. Sometimes I would see a man weeping in front of his Norwegian wife. On other days, I would see a woman from my own neighbourhood shedding tears in the company of a man. A retired professor always had his nose in Schopenhauer. The café was concealed from the embankment by a craft shop trading under the name of *Suffering Moses*. Many years after sauntering along the embankment in Srinagar, I met a woman in London who had been to that shop. She hadn't forgotten its name after eighteen years. "What a name!" she exclaimed, when I mentioned the craft shop to her. The owner of the shop was known throughout the town for his bad temper and revered for his high principles.

Cambridge Station has only one long platform, with the University Press building made of brick on one side and a Royal Mail warehouse made of corrugated metal on the other. The railway station was designed by Sancton Wood in the mid-nineteenth century. It was constructed at a distance from the colleges because the University wanted it to be far from its buildings. We took a bus from the train station to the centre of the town.

Tao Yang had come to Cambridge from Shanghai three years earlier to study English Literature. Her college fees were paid by her parents but she paid for accommodation and food by working in the evenings. There were many students in Cambridge from China and Hong Kong who came from wealthy families. Since the economic reforms of China in the last twenty years, many people had become prosperous and sent their sons and daughters to prestigious universities in other countries. Most students from the Far East took up either Sciences or Business Studies at Cambridge. Tao's choice of English Literature was unusual.

I asked her what it was like to come to Cambridge from Shanghai. She said that she had heard about Cambridge being an idyllic place before her arrival and indeed the town had felt very peaceful to her compared to a big city like Shanghai. At first she liked the idea of the possibilities Cambridge offered her. Then she started to work in a bar where other students came to drink in the evenings and it ruined her illusion of an English idyll. After the bar closed at eleven, Tao worked until midnight cleaning the ashtrays and the floor. She didn't smoke herself but inhaled much smoke exhaled by others. Some of the students found it easier to put out their cigarettes by dipping them in their leftover drinks. The cigarette butts floated effortlessly inside the glasses, turning the clear drinks into a tawny-coloured liquid. Tao would sieve the liquid of its flotsam before loading the glasses into a dishwasher. Her long, smooth hair would smell of cigarettes when she went home from work. So she always took a bath before going to bed at two in the morning.

Tao thought it was a lucky circumstance to be a student in Cambridge after seeing them lounging every night in the bar where she worked. She couldn't empathize with her fellow-students in their protests against the introduction of tuition fees. Her parents had sacrificed everything to pay her fees whereas other students could avail themselves of a long-term loan from the Government. I asked Tao about her job prospects in Shanghai after finishing her degree in Cambridge. She said she could only take up a teaching job in Shanghai and would never be able to pay her parents back from her salary. However, she enjoyed the study of Literature. It gave her consolation. Tao was averse to consumerism. She had very few belongings and, unlike most of the students, she had no inclination to buy the latest CDs or gadgets. She was a friendly person but had no real friends in Cambridge. She knew very well that socializing costs money in a student town.

I found the biblical names of the colleges in Cambridge similar to those in Oxford. However, the landscape was flatter and the town felt spacious. I had first visited Cambridge on a sunny day a few years earlier. Someone asked me if I knew the reason for the unusually fine weather. After a pause, he joked that it was because the students were taking exams. In fact, I saw many students basking on the banks of a languid river. But the sky was overcast on this, my second visit to Cambridge. It was winter and the area behind the colleges, known as the Backs, was desolate. I travelled by bus to the outskirts of the town. There were a few high-tech research centres, recently built in the fields. The sun was setting on the horizon of a flat countryside. The sky was grey but the setting sun produced a flaming red, the image reflected in the glass exterior of a research lab. It was as if a Turner had been reproduced on an immense scale. The scene looked surreal to me.

During my previous visit, I had also been inside the gates of Trinity College to see its library, which was designed by Christopher Wren. On that occasion two or three men were walking across the court, speaking to each other in whispers. I walked around the court to find the entrance of the library. It would have been an intrusion, I thought, to ask someone inside for directions. I entered a smaller court through the Great Court. There were no paths criss-crossing this grass lawn. A sign at its edge read 'Keep off the Grass'. However, a man wearing a bowler hat ignored the sign and walked across the grass. I learnt later that this was a privilege of the senior members of the University.

The library was located on the east side of the court. To enter it, I climbed up a staircase. There were large portraits hanging on the walls at the landing. A courteous elderly lady sitting on a chair by the entrance welcomed me into the library with a nod. The library had a high ceiling and stuccoed walls with ample natural light. Its floor was chequered with black and white tiles. The bookcases formed three-sided enclosures with a table and a few chairs in each bay. Some of the manuscripts in the library were over a thousand years old and the most recent acquisitions of the library dated back to the 1820s. The bookshelves and catalogues were roped off for the use of researchers only.

A chest of drawers used as a catalogue in one of the bays had 'Modern Manuscripts' written on it. I was intrigued by the use of the word 'Modern' in an antiquarian library. Modernism in literature had started many decades after the Wren Library had stopped accepting books. I asked the graceful elderly lady at the entrance about the contents of the catalogue. She was not sure what it meant either.

Marble busts of Trinity men were arranged in a row on either side of the floor, presided over by a full-length statue of Lord Byron. When Vladimir Nabokov was a student at Trinity in the1920s, he never went near its library. His name was not mentioned among the notables of the college in the library leaflet. I asked the elderly lady the reason for this omission. She replied that the college had Milton, Tennyson and Newton among its distinguished alumni. She seemed oblivious of twentieth century names. After a few moments' reflection she remembered that Jawaharlal Nehru – the first Prime Minister of Independent India – had been a student at Trinity.

Pandit Nehru had been to Harrow before joining Trinity. According to his memoirs, he spent his time at Trinity in riding, tennis and gambling rather than politics. He also spent two years in the Inner Temple Hall in London gambling, drinking and running up considerable debts. His grandson, Rajiv Gandhi, joined Trinity half a century later.

A student who looked like a tramp, and whom I had seen in the Great Court, was searching for the manuscript of a children's book. He told me that he studied Sociology at Berkeley University in California. He was very keen to see the manuscript of Newton's *Principia Mathematica* in the library. I wondered why this student from Berkeley was dressed like a tramp when he studied Sociology. I then recalled what Nabokov had written in his autobiography, *Speak Memory*: 'Not once in my three years of Cambridge – not once – did I visit the University Library, or even bother to locate it (I know its new place now), or find out if there existed a college library where books might be borrowed for reading in one's digs. I skipped lectures. I sneaked to London and elsewhere. I conducted several love affairs simultaneously. I had dreadful interviews with Mr Harrison. I translated into Russian a score of poems by Rupert Brooke, *Alice in Wonderland*, and Rolland's *Colas Breugnon*. Scholastically, I might as well have gone up to the Inst. M. M. of Tirana.'

I walked down the staircase to have a look at the façade of the Wren Library. On closer inspection, it turned out to be an ingenious design. The lower semicircular arches were filled to accommodate the bookshelves. The Wren Library is guarded by four statues on the roof which represent Divinity, Law, Physic and Mathematics.

I left Trinity from a gate at the rear into the Backs. The college was flanked by the buildings of two other colleges. Someone told me later that Trinity was the richest college in Cambridge and the third biggest landowner in the country after the Crown and the Church of England.

I hadn't had time to see King's College Chapel on my first visit to Cambridge. But this time I was keen to see Rubens' *Adoration of the Magi*, used as an altarpiece. It was windy outside and when I entered the chapel it felt very warm. The chapel was reverberating with an organ recital. I took a seat to listen to the recital for a few minutes. When I looked up, I saw a very intricate fan-vaulted ceiling. A dark oak screen divided the chapel into two parts. I had been inside a few small chapels before and it was interesting to see a screen between the ante-chapel and the choir. It is an elaborate screen and houses an organ. I entered into the choir through a portal. The altarpiece was glowing in Rubens' vivid colours. It was a very large painting and the alter had been lowered to accommodate it.

I emerged from the warmth of the chapel into the cold air of the front court. The chapel looked long and slender from the outside. I left King's College through the gatehouse and walked along King's Parade towards Trinity Street. The market traders were packing their wares. I searched for the bar where Tao worked in the evenings, cutting through Market Hill to reach St Andrew's Street. Tao, who had gone to her room to drop off her backpack, was already there in her work clothes. It was a modern-looking bar, not very busy in the early evening. Another barmaid was serving a group of Japanese students who sat around a table in one corner. Tao made a coffee for me. It didn't taste as good as the one she made in the café in London; but I didn't expect the coffee served in a bar to taste the same. There were two other groups of students lounging in the bar. One was engaged in a discourse on philosophy. The other students were talking about popular music, showing each other their new CDs. Some of them were going to see a student band from America that was playing at a venue in Cambridge later that evening.

It was from Cambridge that a group of Puritans had left for New England in America during the early seventeenth century. Puritans wished to eliminate elements in the Church of England's liturgy and hierarchy that were reminiscent of Catholicism during the reign of Elizabeth I. The Puritan tradition stressed a suspicion of any state clerical establishment; it wished the church to be a community of visible saints, sharply differentiated from 'the ungodly'; and it emphasized the ministry of the word – the Bible and the sermon. But it was their claim to uniquely extreme personal piety and high seriousness that earned the Puritans their name. The Pilgrim Fathers who sailed to Massachusetts carried copies of the Cambridge Bible with them. They laid the foundation of a new town near the Boston area and called it Cambridge in honour of their Alma Mater. A college was founded in 1636 and named after its first benefactor, John Harvard. The college offered a classic academic course based on the Cambridge University model but consistent with the Puritan philosophy of the first colonists.

John Harvard was a Cambridge man who had graduated from Emmanuel College. He was the son of a butcher from Southwark in South London. He arrived in New England as a clergyman and died of consumption at the age of thirty-one. He bequeathed his collection of books and a few hundred pounds to the college named after him. Eighty years after his death, another colonist made a big contribution to a different college in New Haven. The name of the benefactor was Elihu Yale and the college was renamed after him. Yale had worked for the East India Company as a governor of Madras, amassing great wealth through private trading while working for 'the Honourable Company'. He spent twenty-seven years in India. Because of the scandals concerning his administration, he was removed from his post in 1692 and returned to London a few years later.

On my first visit to Cambridge, a bus tour took me a few miles out of town to an American War Cemetery located on the slope of a hill on land donated by the University of Cambridge. A towering flagpole was flying a bright American flag. The headstones were cross-shaped and laid out in concentric rows. There was a chapel at the far end of the cemetery. The door of the chapel had gunboats and artillery carved on it. I found this place of worship very militaristic and left the site quickly.

As it turned darker, the bar became busier. Tao was juggling with emptying and loading the dishwasher with glasses and ashtrays. She was very quick on her feet. She had told me earlier that she felt so exhausted at midnight when she finished work that it took her twenty minutes to walk home. I asked her why she didn't ride a bike. Tao said that she had bought a bike when she came to Cambridge but it was stolen three months later outside her home. She bought a new bike and it was stolen near her college a few days later. She always chained it to a fence but the thieves had broken the lock. So she decided not to buy a bicycle again. I had assumed that, unlike London, there were no bicycle thieves in Cambridge. I saw bicycles everywhere in the town and because some of them had rickety wheels I thought that many students had abandoned them after leaving the town – until I saw a few of them riding rusty bikes. Tao told me that in fact bicycle theft was very common in Cambridge. This was especially disappointing to her because, as a little girl, she had heard stories from her grandfather about the existence of 'honesty bookshops' in various towns in England where passers-by picked up a book and put their money in a box. Her grandfather had worked for an Englishman in Shanghai as a domestic servant until World War II.

Shanghai was the creation of British business interests in the area. The first foreign settlement was established there in 1843 following a treaty. The East India Company was sending large quantities of opium to China. Like cotton and spices, opium was one of its main trading commodities. The Company had assumed the monopoly of opium-growing in Bengal in the eighteenth century. The opium was sold at auction in Calcutta and smuggled into China. The Company ships did not carry it because the Emperor had banned its sale. But the cash they received from the auction was laundered through London or Calcutta. Opium was a valued medicine that could deaden pain and assist sleep, but it was also habit-forming and many people in China became addicted. The East India Company's trade monopoly was abolished in 1834, but the smuggling of opium into China by European private traders intensified. The Chinese state was deeply disturbed at this and threatened force. Britain was prepared to defend 'free trade' and in 1840 they went to war. The outcome was defeat for the Chinese and a treaty which ceded Hong Kong to the British.

The French and Americans followed the British in obtaining concessions in the port of Shanghai. The city became well-known for its role as the base of European imperialism in mainland China. Shanghai has the largest array of Art Deco architecture in the world. The British built grand buildings along the waterfront known as the Bund – an Anglo-Indian word for embankment. While growing up in Srinagar, I liked to stroll along its Bund, passing a toll-house on my way from the old town to the splendours of the Raj in the British quarter of our town. One day an elderly resident told me that he had been fearful to walk beyond the toll-house during his childhood when a British Sahib was in residence in a colonial house there. A racecourse was built near the Bund in Shanghai but it was a forbidden place for the Chinese population. Some people referred to the Shanghai of the early twentieth century as 'the Paris of the

East', whereas others called it 'the demi-mondaine of the Orient'.

Tao told me that Shanghai had been undergoing rapid expansion during the last twenty years. A 'New Bund' was being built across the river in Pudong. When Tao had arrived in Cambridge from Shanghai, she found it rather a sleepy town. She told me that there was a place in New Town in Shanghai known as Cambridge Forest. There was an increase, she said, in the number of Chinese students attending various colleges in Cambridge in the last twenty years. Many of them came from families who had risen in the recent economic boom and liked their children to be educated either at Cambridge or the London School of Economics. There was actually an association for Chinese students in Cambridge. It offered a haircutting service for as little as three pounds and cyclists could borrow a pump from their office, which had a footstand like the ones used in China. Tao did not participate in the activities of the association. She didn't have time for socializing in Cambridge because she had to work in the evenings to make ends meet.

I was more struck by the similarities of Oxford and Cambridge than the differences between the two towns. The architecture of the towns had the same signatures – those of Christopher Wren and James Gibbs. Wren, who was an astronomer and a scientist, designed his first building in Cambridge as a college chapel. His next building was the

Sheldonian Theatre in Oxford. James Gibbs designed the Radcliffe Camera in Oxford and the Senate House in Cambridge. When I saw the various buildings in Oxford and Cambridge made of stone, I began to understand why universities elsewhere were called 'redbrick'. The rivers of both towns have been given poetic names – the Thames is 'Isis', the Cam is 'Granta'. If Oxford boasts about the number of British Prime Ministers it has educated, Cambridge takes pride in the many Nobel laureates among its alumni. Oxford has given birth to the new denomination of Methodism, while Emmanuel College in Cambridge has bred Puritanism. There is a network of canals in both towns and each town had its own Bridge of Sighs. Punting is a form of recreation in both Oxford and Cambridge. And, of course, they both like to beat each other in their annual boat race.

For many years, I had cherished the unrealistic idea of leaving London and living in Oxford or Cambridge for a few months in order to write a book. However, after visiting these towns a few times it seemed absurd for me to move there. I felt out of place in a university town. The old institutions of Oxford and Cambridge have inspired admiration in many colonial people who saw them as seats of power. In the end, I rejected the idea of finding inspiration for writing in either of them.

I boarded a train in Cambridge at eight o'clock in the evening and reached London in forty-five minutes. King's

Cross Station looked imposing in the evening light, with many people heading towards the entrance of St Pancras Station. It dawned on me that this Gothic building was very similar to the Victoria Terminus in Bombay, built during the time of the Raj. The Ring Road was very busy with buses and lorries. One or two streetwalkers were soliciting on the other side of the road. A group of men who were living rough sat on the pavement near the entrance of a fast food restaurant. The area retained its character despite the local regeneration projects. I was happy to find my bicycle still there, chained to a fence. I avoided the busy Euston Road, preferring to cut through Somerstown to reach home.

I visited Cambridge again a week later to better acquaint myself with it as I had spent just a few hours there on my previous visit. It got dark early in January and I could only obtain an overview of the town. I also wanted to meet Tao when she was not at work. So I arrived in Cambridge just before noon. I tried to locate a bookshop near Market Hill where I had bought an out-of-print book a few years earlier but I had trouble finding it again. However, I saw two new bookshops very close to each other in the same street. It took me a little while to realize that the bookshop I'd been seeking, which sold both new and second-hand books, had probably closed down. I walked down Trinity Street to be certain that I hadn't missed the shop and discovered another bookshop instead. It was enjoyable to browse in this bookshop with its individual character rather than the chain bookshops of uniform international appearance. On leaving the bookshop, I saw a circular building further down the road, which turned out – unusually for its shape – to be a church. I also discovered the home of the Cambridge Union Society behind the rotunda.

I met Tao in a pizzeria at the corner of Market Hill. She was accompanied by a friend from Beijing whom she had met at her college in Cambridge. They had been to a grocery and were carrying a few shopping bags. When she first arrived in Cambridge, Tao had worked in a Chinese restaurant for a few months. She was surprised to find that diners usually tipped the waitress in British restaurants. People in China, she told me, often paid *less* than the amount on their restaurant bill. Despite the bonus of tips, she had found it tough to work in a Chinese restaurant in Cambridge.

Tao had been to Chinatown in London a few times. She was dismayed to see that Chinese men and women who worked in the restaurants in this neighbourhood often gambled in one of the two casinos around there. Many years ago I had met in Chinatown an Englishman called John who spoke Mandarin. He taught English in a language school in the West End. Sometimes John would hang around a pagoda in Chinatown and, like a sleuth, would eavesdrop. He told me one day that there were Chinese peasants usually loitering near the pagoda waiting to be hired as restaurant hands. He would also pick up information about the activities of triads in Gerrard Street. John had been a bus driver before becoming an English teacher. He had also been to the Far East a few times. He had wanted to bring a woman from a village in Thailand to London but found it difficult to convince the British Consulate over there that he could support her. He collected the cards of Oriental girls displayed in the phone boxes in Central London. John went to a Chinese hairdresser above a shop in Wardour Street. The hairdresser had confided to him that he paid some money to a triad now and again for running a salon in Chinatown. According to John, the triads demanded money only from the Chinese businessmen in the West End and would leave others alone. He bought buns and rolls for his afternoon tea from a bakery in Gerrard Street. He spoke to the owner of the bakery in Mandarin and she would give him a discount. John also knew a herbalist in Chinatown and would recommend him to his students. A few of them worked in various restaurants in Chinatown and sometimes brought food for him to take home. It was amusing to hear him speak Mandarin to his students.

Tao and her friend liked to shop in a market in Cambridge where traders offered their wares at discounted prices. They mostly bought dry food such as noodles at a grocery. Because her kitchen was not fitted with a cooker Tao found it easier to prepare a meal of noodles at home just by adding water. She used a microwave oven to warm up the food. Many students in Cambridge were very health-conscious and spent time in jogging and swimming. But Tao could not find time for any recreational activity apart from going to the cinema once or twice a month. She was resigned to her fate of being a student from a poor country. Students from a rich country like America had a different perspective, complaining about all sorts of things in Cambridge. A few of them had told her that they found the place very inefficient and felt exasperated by the amount of paperwork required for simple things.

After leaving the pizzeria, Tao and her friend obliged me by guiding me on a walking tour. We walked along St Mary's Passage towards King's Parade. Tao told me that the building in front of us was Senate House, where the graduation ceremonies are held in summer. A costumier opposite Senate House supplied gowns and headgear to the graduates for these ceremonies. The pavement signboard of the shop was painted in Cambridge Blue, the same light blue colour used on a few other shop fronts in Cambridge. Next to the costumier was a tearoom known as Auntie's Teashop, which had china displayed in wooden cabinets. I was pleased to see that because when I was little I used to call my mother 'auntie'. But it was not unusual for children in Kashmir to call their mother either 'sister' or 'auntie'.

Tao wanted to show me Downing Street. So we turned into Pembroke Street, which becomes Downing Street. There were various museums on both sides of the road, including one of archaeology and anthropology which Tao wanted me to see in order to understand the topography of Cambridgeshire. I was surprised to discover that it displayed artefacts gathered by Captain Cook on his first voyage to the South Pacific.

I had heard about the landscape of the county being referred to as the Fens. However, it was in the museum that I came to learn that the vast marshland to the north of Cambridge was systematically drained in the seventeenth century and that Ely was an island within an island until then. The museum covered Roman Britain in one of its galleries on the ground floor. Romans has arrived in this part of Britain two thousand years ago and built the town that would eventually be called Cambridge. They had also built a road connecting Cambridge to Colchester. On my visit to the museum it became obvious to me why they called a mound a hill in Cambridge. It would have appeared a hill only to a fensman.

After leaving the museum we wandered around Corpus Christi College and then took a narrow lane towards Market Hill. The wind made it inhospitable for us to roam the streets so we entered a coffee-shop for a hot drink. The coffee-shop was part of the same chain for which Tao worked in London and it was a useful hideaway for me.

Stratford-upon-Shakespeare

For many years while growing up in Kashmir, I believed Shakespeare's *Hamlet* was a small village in England without a church, not a Danish prince. However, I was lucky not to be forced to read Shakespeare at school as hatred of the Bard mostly begins in the classroom. In fact, the English dramatist had found an ardent follower in the unlikely location of Srinagar. Our neighbour there held court among the artisans and recited *Macbeth* and *King Lear* in front of them like a thespian. Sometimes I would hear him declaring "Fair is foul, and foul is fair" to his bewildered audience. Some people thought he was insane, whereas others thought it profane of him to quote a Catholic playwright rather than Imam Ali. And like a graceful actor he always took his leave with a memorable line from one of Shakespeare's plays.

The first time I went to a theatre in London was when a kindly lady whom I served in a shop in Hampstead offered me a free ticket to see her production of *Brief Candle* performed in a small theatre in the neighbourhood. Walking up the hill after finishing work, I met someone who was also going there. He asked me if I was into plays. As a child, I had seen people going to the theatre only in Hindi movies.

A group of sophisticated people had already gathered at the entrance of this small theatre. I felt awkward at entering a playhouse for the first time in London on a free ticket. But it was a joy to watch an accomplished actor play miscellaneous roles in the play. Well-built, and with a commanding voice, he was a versatile actor who had worked for the Royal Shakespeare Company for some time. A few days after seeing the play I learned that the woman who had given me a free ticket was in fact his wife. Remembering her kindness, I felt sad when I read his obituary in a newspaper a few years later.

I summoned up courage one evening to go to see *Hamlet* in a theatre at the Barbican Centre. I had failed to understand the absence of Shakespeare's plays in the West End. It was the location of the Barbican and not the length of the play that I found daunting. It was actually an American woman who gave me inspiration to go to the Barbican by accompanying me there. Although she was very young, her understanding of Shakespeare was profound. I was surprised to see the play set in the modern corporate world with Claudius in an Italian suit as chairman of the board. At last I began to understand the lines that had baffled me in my childhood.

It was the last season of the Royal Shakespeare Company at the Barbican and they began touring the country a few months later. When I mentioned the play next day to my workmates they looked at me askance. It dawned on me that Shakespeare was not much liked at home.

The RSC had found a venue in the Round House near Chalk Farm for a few months. It was just down the road from where I lived, which gave me a chance to see a few more plays during their residency. The seats in the theatre were uncomfortable but the price of the tickets was very reasonable. A theatre critic who sat next to me at one of the performances found it difficult to fit into a single seat. She was taking notes during the play and didn't seem to enjoy the performance. I was bothered by her restlessness. The staff in the theatre paid due attention to her, knowing she was going to review the play in a national newspaper.

I wanted to book a room for a night in Stratford-upon-Avon before booking a seat for a performance at the Royal Shakespeare Theatre. I found the phone number of a small guesthouse described as pleasant in a guidebook. I rang the guesthouse to find out if they had a room available for one night. The lady who answered told me they were not very busy and offered me a room at a rate much lower than I expected. She asked me my time of arrival. I took it for a standard question but then the lady told me that she was looking after her elderly mother and usually attended to her once or twice in the afternoon. I was touched by her concern for an elderly mother. I had already checked the train timetable and told her I was going to arrive in town around one o'clock.

I left home in the morning just in time to catch the right train to Stratford. I had decided to ride my old rusty bike and leave it outside Marylebone station for the night. After riding it for a few yards, I tried to check the brakes and got thrown off the bike, bruising my right hand. I reached Marylebone Station on time, but the train had already departed and the next train wasn't due for two hours. I phoned the lady at the guesthouse and let her know about the delay. She was grateful that I called and told me that she was volunteering in a charity shop for an hour from four to five o'clock.

I took a seat in a café inside the station and wondered what to do for the next two hours. I suddenly remembered a colonnaded building across the road which housed a library – an ideal place to spend some time. I liked the cupola of its reading-room and the wooden pillars that support its ceiling. Time passed very quickly in the reading room for me, so quickly that I suddenly realized that the next train to Stratford was departing in a few minutes and I had to rush back to the station. Just before boarding the train, I spotted a bicycle rack along the platform. I needn't have bruised myself by riding a rusty old bike as it would have been quite safe to leave my new bike inside the station for a night.

The station at Stratford-upon-Avon is built in the shape of a manor house with a few chimneys rising above its roof. I walked to the guesthouse, which was located only a short distance from the station. A car rental company's office outside the station heralded Stratford as a touristy town. The town centre was well signposted. I passed a hotel called Victoria on my way, its appearance indeed reminiscent of Victorian times, and saw a sign for the road leading to my accommodation. There were many B&B's along the road advertising vacancies on signboards hanging in their windows. Many of them were named after Shakespeare's plays. The small dining-rooms of these guesthouses were crammed with furniture. I hoped my accommodation would be a bit more spacious.

I rang the doorbell of the guesthouse and waited for a few minutes before ringing again. The door opened and I was greeted by the lady to whom I had spoken on the phone. She was energetic, slim and grey-haired. She pointed out the breakfast room on the ground floor before showing me a bedroom on the first floor. It was a Victorian-style house with a creaky staircase covered by a carpet of floral design.

I was uncertain about where my landlady was from after speaking to her for a few minutes. Our conversation was interrupted when her phone rang and she left the room to answer the call. She appeared again a few minutes later and told me that she was from Colorado in America. But she had neutralized her native accent so effectively that I could not guess her origin when I spoke to her on the phone. However, her openness had made me wonder whether she might be American.

She told me her name was Jenny and she was sixty years old. Her mother, whom she looked after, was ninety. The guesthouse belonged to her sister, who had gone to Wales for a few days. Jenny had been teaching English to Navajo children for fourteen years and wanted to find a new job after going back to Colorado, but being sixty years old, she considered the prospects of finding another job slim. Her sister had paid her travel expenses to fly from America to look after the business while she was away. She liked to keep herself busy. She cleaned the rooms for guests, prepared breakfast for them in the morning and also washed the bed linen.

Jenny asked me to order breakfast for the morning. When I told her I just wanted some cereal and milk, she said it meant she didn't have to cook breakfast for me. It seemed odd to use the verb 'cook' in conjunction with breakfast. Jenny was shortly going to her voluntary work in the charity shop. She handed me a map of the town before rushing out of the house.

I was glad that the room was not crammed with furniture. There was a wicker chair padded with a cushion in the room. The teapot and cups placed on a small table were made of fine china. The bed linen had the light fragrance of washing powder.

I left the guesthouse to go to the Royal Shakespeare Theatre and collect my ticket from the box office. I had always thought that the name 'box office' strictly applied to the cabin in the foyer of a theatre where tickets are usually sold. Then one day a Shakespearian actress told me that the phrase originally came from the box placed inside a room in which the audience deposited their money during Elizabethan times. I walked along Waterside towards Bridge Street trying to find the theatre, before asking someone for directions – who told me that the theatre was right behind me. I turned around and saw a forbidding brick structure flying the red flags of the RSC. A pair of swans sculpted in stainless steel was mounted on a fountain in a park in front of the theatre. A flock of real Canadian geese swam in the water nearby.

The woman at the box office offered me a better seat, saying that the theatre was not too busy. There were still a few hours to go before the evening performance. I decided to see a bit more of the town. Besides the RST, there was a theatre called The Swan which was smaller but pleasing to the eye. The theatre was 'dark' that night. I took Sheep Street towards Market Place, which I had passed on my way to the RST. Many buildings had half-timbered facades fitted with mullion windows. I felt as if I had travelled back in time.

When I reached Ely Street, I saw a man in country gear and headphones walking back and forth with a sandwich-board strapped to him that advertised an antiques centre. It was late afternoon but I didn't see many tourists around. I turned a corner and came upon Harvard House, which belongs to Harvard University in America. I had seen pictures of this house flying an American flag, but now I only saw a bare flagpole protruding like a rhino's horn from its top floor. I found a hotel known as The White Swan near the Market Place. It had existed there as an inn before the time of Shakespeare. I also found the charity shop where Jenny worked in the afternoon. She had told me that it was in front of the American Fountain. I was puzzled by this name until I learnt that it was the gift of George W. Childs, a journalist from Philadelphia. It was built during Queen Victoria's Golden Jubilee in 1887. Since I started travelling out of London, I had found something American in every English town I visited.

I drifted back towards the River Avon before the start of the play. Unsure if I could find somewhere to eat after the performance ended, I decided to eat before going to the theatre. I found a nearby restaurant serving fish and chips. When I went inside to enquire about their opening times, the man frying fish behind the counter told me that they were closing at 7 o'clock. He reminded me of Kasim the kiosk vendor in London. I was surprised to find a North African working in a fish and chips restaurant in Stratford-upon-Avon. I ordered scampi and chips but the fish didn't taste as good as the equivalent I sometimes ate in a London restaurant.

I left the restaurant to go to the theatre across the road. There were a few men and women in formal clothes walking towards the RST. One of the women was wearing a blue velvety coat. The foyer was full of distinguished-looking people who spoke in hushed tones. The theatre looked as big as a cinema auditorium in India. It had over a thousand seats, which gradually filled. But there were not many foreign tourists among the audience. It seemed that most of them came from other English counties to see the play. It was not one of Shakespeare's plays that was to be performed that evening but an anthology piece called *The Hollow Crown*, written by John Barton, a co-founder of the RSC. I would have liked to see one of Shakespeare's plays in his hometown, but both the Swan and The Other Place were closed that night.

The play was an inane recitation of the history of Kings and Queens of England. I was not too keen to hear a lecture on the English monarchy in a theatre in Stratford when I could have stayed at home and watched it on television. I would have left the theatre after half an hour but the fine rendition of the actors kept me there until the end. I was glad there was a twenty-minute interval. I felt the need to breathe fresh air outside the theatre while others were eating their ice creams in the foyer.

After leaving the theatre I took a walk through the town to reach the guesthouse and found a few restaurants along the way that were open after 10 o'clock. But most of them were empty. I wondered if there was a train leaving for London at that time of the evening and wished I had checked the timetable earlier. But it was time for me to overcome my fear of spending a night outside London. The habit of going home for the night was deeply rooted in me. As a child I would sometimes agree to spend a night at my grandma's house in Srinagar and then in the middle of the night would insist on going home. My grandma would send me home with one of my uncles, who carried a lantern to find the way in the dark. It was hard for me as a child to fall asleep in a bedroom that was not my own and then wake up in the morning in unfamiliar surroundings.

Having picked up a leaflet at the RST for a walking tour of the town, I wanted to start early in the morning to be there on time. But it took me a while to let go of my old habit and fall asleep in a guesthouse room. The whistling of water running in the pipes kept me awake for some time. It made a choking sound whenever the tap was turned on or off in another room.

There were two more guests having breakfast in the dining-room in the morning. Jenny had laid a table for them in one corner of the room. When I saw their breakfast, I realized that Jenny must have cooked a few items for them. It was bizarre to find an American woman hosting an English couple in Stratford-upon-Avon. Jenny asked me if I wanted any fried eggs or baked beans. I ordered some toast instead. She was happy that at least I had asked her for that.

I had asked Jenny on my arrival the previous day about

the check-out time. She told me it was 10 am, not midday like most of the hotels in London. I asked her if I could leave my bag with her until I caught my train to London in the afternoon. She said that she'd be out during the afternoon but her sister, who was coming back from Wales around noon, would be there.

I left the guesthouse in the morning and walked towards the fountain with its pair of mounted metal swans, the starting point of the walking tour. A few large coaches full of tourists could be seen in town but when I arrived at the fountain I found no one else there waiting for the tour. Eventually I saw a few people coming towards me looking for the tour guide. He arrived soon and introduced himself as a local resident.

The guide began his tour with a lecture on the Royal Shakespeare Theatre. He thought the building was an eyesore. The District Council wanted to rebuild it but the plan had met with resistance from the locals who formed a group know as 'HOOT', an acronym for Hands Off Our Theatre. The guide said that the council had later decided to alter the theatre only on the inside, leaving its exterior intact. It was the exterior rather than the interior of the theatre which struck me as a bad example of cinema-hall architecture. The guide moved on to the historical importance of the canal basin for Stratford and mentioned a recent flood that had engulfed part of the town.

We followed the guide along Chapel Street towards

Market Place, from where he led us to Shakespeare's birthplace museum in Henley Street. It looked like a replica house in a tidy film set. It was teeming with tourists – many of them schoolchildren from far-off countries. The crowd in Henley Street gave me some idea how many people visited Stratford every day. The guide told us that he had seen an increasing number of tourists coming from countries belonging to the former Soviet Union.

Shakespeare was writing *Hamlet* when the East India Company men set sail on their maiden voyage. It surprised me to learn that he had remained obscure at home for so many years. But his reputation in the world at large was established with the expansion of the British Empire. Walking down the crowded Henley Street, it occurred to me that Shakespeare had contributed to the imperial enterprise more than anyone else. How, otherwise, could *Macbeth* and *King Lear* be performed in Zulu and in Kathakali style in the twenty-first century?

There was a group of schoolchildren from France visiting the museum. If France had colonised as many countries as Britain then perhaps Racine's reputation in Asia and Africa would have been as great as that of Shakespeare. I had seen Racine's *Phèdre* performed in a theatre in London only once in ten years. The French, who had initially found Shakespeare too vulgar to be translated into their language, seemed to have given in to his reputation lately. Proust did not like it that his translator, Scott Moncrieff, borrowed a line from a Shakespeare sonnet for the English title of his work. He wrote a letter saying, 'the lines you add, the dedications to your friends, are no substitute for the ambiguity of temps perdu' – the 'dedication to your friends' being, of course, the first two lines of a Shakespeare sonnet.

Our guide thought Henley Street the right place to tell his audience more about various theories as to who was the real Shakespeare. One of the theories stipulated that Shakespeare had travelled around the world with Francis Drake before settling in London to write plays. Being a Stratford man, the guide did not care for the views of anti-Stratfordians. He was not convinced by their postulations and tried to hold on to whatever little was known about the life of Stratford's most famous son.

I was puzzled to learn about the enigma of Shakespeare for the first time. It was intriguing that someone whose work was central to an entire civilization had eluded historians regarding the details of his own life. Shakespeare is regarded by many as the greatest writer in the English language, and it is easy to mistake him for the greatest writer in any language if one lives in a Commonwealth country. I had heard Shakespeare's name a long time before I became acquainted with Ovid, from whose work Shakespeare borrowed ideas for his plays.

After visiting the museum, the guide led us to Holy Trinity Church, where Shakespeare is buried. We walked along Southern Lane, passing a theatre known as The Other

Place. Its name reminded me of Oxford, where people like to refer to Cambridge as 'the other place'. The 13th century church looked even older than it was. Its doorway was very low and one had to bend down to enter. When I read the inscription, 'and curst be he that moves my bones', on Shakespeare's grave, I understood why it was also known as the cursed tomb. It was inside this church that our guide elucidated the subject of persecution of Catholics in Elizabethan England and Shakespeare's hidden catholic self in his work. I thought of our neighbour in Srinagar who, perhaps as a Shia Muslim in predominantly Sunni Kashmir, understood Shakespeare's work better than the majority of people there. Shakespeare the actor had entertained the English monarch, who was responsible for the persecution of the Catholics. He must have kept his faith secret. This was in fact one of the tenets of Shia belief: to keep one's faith hidden when living among a hostile majority.

We left Holy Trinity Church to see other places of interest. The guide led us to what is known as New Place, where a big house once stood in which Shakespeare spent his last years. According to some, the cause of his death at the age of fifty-two was alcohol, since they believe that Shakespeare, living a solitary life in the inns of London, had turned to drink. Nothing much has survived of New Place except the foundation of an old house. We followed the guide into an enclosed garden behind it. There were sculptures in the garden based on Shakespeare's characters. It was a desolate place, except for a tramp reclining against the pedestal of a sculpture with a bottle in his hand. The guide pointed out the school opposite this garden, which Shakespeare is believed to have attended. Many of Shakespeare's contemporaries went to universities that only took single men. Shakespeare, who at eighteen had married Anne Hathaway when she was already three months pregnant, had been barred.

We passed an almshouse built in Tudor-style, like many buildings in Stratford. Further down the road was The Shakespeare Hotel, apparently an authentic period survival. The guide also showed us the house where Shakespeare's son-in-law, a prominent Stratford man, had lived. Our tour finished at the American Fountain where the guide bade us farewell.

After stopping in a coffee-shop, I went back to Henley Street to see the museum. When I entered the museum shop, I saw the woman with whom I had shared a café table that day, working behind the counter. She acknowledged me with a humorous greeting and directed me to the entrance of the museum next door.

Visitors had to walk through an exhibition which tried to recreate Shakespeare's obscure life in Stratford-upon-Avon. This passage to the house was blocked by a large group of schoolchildren and I had to wait for some time to get in. A room on the ground floor had leather gloves hanging in the window – Shakespeare's father is supposed to have been a glove-maker. I had heard from someone that in fact he was a butcher. An attendant in the room mentioned to me that in the gravediggers' scene in *Hamlet* Shakespeare has used his knowledge of the tanning trade. He said that Shakespeare had also compared the conscience of a man to a hide because of its suppleness. I asked the attendant about the textiles and the furniture in the museum. He told me that the interior was based on Dutch paintings of that period because it was difficult to find English paintings of the same era.

I drifted into a modern glass and iron building which houses The Shakespeare Centre. I would have liked to see the vast collection of books on Shakespeare in the Centre but unfortunately it was not open to the public. I had therefore to be content with the display of artworks based on Shakespeare's verse in the foyer of the building.

The Royal Mail issued a set of postage stamps a few years ago to commemorate the opening of Shakespeare's Globe in London. I was glad to see the picture of this thatch-roofed theatre on the stamps. But it took me a few years to make the trip across London Bridge to see the Globe. One day, while walking along Bankside, I bought a standing ticket to see *Twelfth Night* there. It was an all-male production in which men were dressed up as women. The play transported me back to my schooldays in Kashmir where a play was performed for us by amateur actors on a makeshift stage. The role of the mother was played by a man wearing a burka. It was easy for him to convince us of his role by keeping his face concealed under the veil. The male actors performing in

Twelfth Night had applied ample cosmetics to look feminine. The audience laughed loudly at their gestures but not at their words. They seemed to be more stirred by the costumes than Shakespeare's blank verse. I felt distracted by their laughter and the noise of the aeroplanes crossing the sky above the theatre.

I returned to the Globe a few years later to see an exhibition. It was surprising to learn that this reconstruction had come about as a result of many years' dedicated effort by an American actor-director, Sam Wanamaker. I met a man wearing a yarmulke in the exhibition. He told me that he was from Dallas in America and was visiting London only for a few days. He was here to find out why Shakespeare had chosen a Jewish moneylender as the main character in one of his plays when there were no Jews living in England, having been expelled long before his time. He said that he was, nevertheless, an admirer of Shakespeare's works.

I went back to the guesthouse in Stratford to pick up my bag. It was Jenny's brother-in-law who opened the door and let me in, a native Stratford man, I was told. I left the guesthouse to go to the train station and again noticed rows of guesthouses along the way.

The next train to London was departing in half an hour so I sat in a waiting room until it arrived. There were plenty of vacant seats in the train. But that morning I had seen hordes of tourists arriving in the town by coach. This small town of a hundred thousand people received about half a million tourists a year. Most of them visited the town because of Shakespeare's fame, though they were not always quite familiar with his works. Stratford is also a place of pilgrimage for those who perform in his plays, which have been translated into nearly a hundred languages. I remembered a Macedonian girl I'd met in Henley Street during the walking tour telling me that her mother wouldn't let her go out to play when she was young until she'd read a little of Shakespeare's work. Thus, Macedonia, which produced Alexander the Great in the third century BC, has yielded to an English dramatist in the twenty-first century.

Hay-on-Wye Fever

I heard the name 'Hay-on-Wye' for the first time from someone who owned a shop there. It wasn't a bookshop but a clothing shop. She also owned a similar shop in the neighbourhood in London where I lived. The name of the town sounded fanciful to me. The first word of this compound place-name was simple but the last one was elusive. It reminded me of Manzoor from Lake Dal in Srinagar, who often taught his friends how to say 'Wales' by rounding his lips and trying to distinguish it from the sound of the word 'vales'. Manzoor told me once that the Welsh landscape is beautiful. Being a guide, he had heard it from British men and women travelling in India. Manzoor also told me that there was a man from Srinagar living in London who travelled to Wales at weekends. The idea of spending weekends in another town suggested that this person was prosperous. When I eventually met him in West London a few years later, he turned out to be a broken man.

Walking along Charing Cross Road in London once, I saw a sign posted on the window of a second-hand bookshop which said:

> 'Tomorrow our books will fly
> From London to Hay-on-Wye'

I was curious to visit the place where those second-hand books were destined to land. The lady who owned the shop there had told me not to visit the town during its literary festival since it becomes very crowded. When I asked her if I could go there on a day trip, she told me it would be impossible to get there and back to London the same day. The train didn't go all the way there and the bus service between Hereford and Hay-on-Wye was infrequent. It seemed easier to travel to Paris from London by train and be back by the evening than this remote-looking town on the border of England and Wales.

I wanted to catch a direct train from Paddington to Hereford just before midday, which meant that I'd have to wait only an hour in Hereford to board the next bus to Hay-on-Wye. If I caught an earlier train, I'd have to wait two hours for the bus. I had even considered cycling from Hereford to Hay-on-Wye but the distance was a bit too long for a bike ride. I secured my bicycle with a pair of locks outside Paddington station for an overnight journey out of London. There inside the station was the children's storybook character, Paddington Bear, cast in bronze. An automated message recorded in a voice that dropped at the end of each port of call greeted the passengers as soon as the train left the station. The announcer stated that passengers could buy tea or coffee at a counter in one of the carriages. After a while, I made my way towards that carriage to get a coffee. However, their coffee machine was broken and it was going to be a long journey without a hot drink. I was glad to find a sign designating my carriage as 'QUIET' – forbidding the use of mobile phones. I sank in a seat at the end of the coach with my nose in a travel book, *Tigers in Red Weather*, which made my journey seem shorter.

The train arrived in Hereford on time. I wanted to confirm the departure time of the bus to Hay-on-Wye before wandering around the town for an hour, so I walked towards the bus station to have a look at the timetable. There were a few people sitting in the shelter waiting for a bus. I asked someone about the next bus to Hay-on-Wye. He gave me the route number and told me to check the timetable on the wall. I had enough time to see a bit of Hereford. There was a coffee-shop nearby, apparently a haunt for pensioners. The coffee was inexpensive, very milky and tasted like the instant variety. But I was desperate for a hot drink.

I was able to see nothing noteworthy in my short excursion around town and returned to the bus station fifteen minutes before the scheduled departure of the next bus as I didn't want to miss it and be stranded in Hereford for two more hours. The bus arrived a few minutes early but its driver told the people waiting at the station that he was taking it out of service. He instructed us to wait for the later bus, the last one that day to Hay-on-Wye. If this one was also taken out of service, then I would be stranded in Hereford until next morning.

The people waiting at the station dispersed quietly. I wanted to find a library in town to spend the waiting time there. On the way, I discovered a fine cathedral and admired the varied colours of its stonework. The library, also housed in a stone building, occupied the ground floor, whereas the upper floors served as a museum, where a Roman mosaic was displayed on one of the walls that formed the stairwell.

I returned to the bus station after leaving the library and loitered in the town for some time. It was a relief when the last bus to Hay-on-Wye finally arrived. At last I was able to depart.

The bus moved through the town gently and then sped along a narrow road flanked by high bushes. It would have been difficult for me to cycle along this road with the prospect of being chased by a speeding bus. No cars or lorries were driving along this road but I saw one or two horse riders waiting on one side, giving way to our bus, which was full as it was the last one that day. Many of the passengers were youngsters returning home from school in Hereford.

Naturally, I wanted to see the celebrated second-hand bookshops in Hay-on-Wye. The other reason for me to visit was to see the Black Mountains overlooking the town. I also carried in my mind a photograph of the town that had probably been taken from a distance on a fine day. Its colours reminded me of Vermeer's *View of Delft*.

I got off the bus near the castle. The literary festival had finished several days earlier but its banner was still up. The entrance to the festival site, teeming with people in newspaper pictures, looked desolate. An industrial-size marquee was pitched nearby. It looked as if two marquees had been pitched side by side and one of them had been taken down. The carpet had discoloured a big square of grass. There were pallets, empty crates and other leftover items heaped up on one side of the ground. A narrow passage led to the castle, which housed a second-hand bookshop – still open – on its ground floor. The town was laid out around the castle.

I looked for the way to the Old Black Lion where I had booked a room. It was six o'clock and, judging from the empty streets, the town residents had already retired for the night. I found a shop which was still open and asked a woman there for directions. The kindly lady handed me a copy of the local map and explained how to get to the Old Black Lion. The map showed all the bookshops in the town. I was not sure if it was a leftover from the festival or if shops in Hay obliged passers-by with a copy of this map throughout the year.

I had already forgotten the directions given by the lady as I left the shop. I took a leisurely walk, knowing that it was a small town and my chances of getting lost here were minimal. The town appeared deserted, except for people sitting at picnic tables outside a pub. I saw a sign for Lion Street and knew that I was close to the tavern. When I turned a corner, I saw the whitewashed exterior of a seventeenth-century building with flower baskets hanging outside. Its name intrigued me. I had heard about black leopards but a black lion seemed imaginary, like Borges' blue tigers.

The entrance led to the bar through a side door. I went into the bar section to check in. Two men standing in front of the bar waiting for a drink greeted me, thinking that I had also come in for a drink. The barman asked me what I would like after serving them. When I told him that I had reserved a room the other two men smiled. They had seen me queuing up behind them and made a remark about the British habit of forming a queue, thereby including me among them. They thought I had arrived in the town by car. When I told them that I'd travelled by bus they were taken by surprise. One of them remarked that it must have been an adventure.

The barman volunteered to show me the room while handing me the keys. I followed him up the stairs. The room allocated to me had such a low door that one could enter it only by lowering one's head. It reminded me of the houses in an old part of Srinagar, built with very low doorways, it was said, to make it difficult for invading Afghan horsemen to ransack these houses. It also brought to mind a recent film in which the main character lived on a floor in a multi-storied building, its ceiling just four feet high due to an architectural error. There was a step between the hallway and the room, which was small but with neat décor. The barman showed me a separate bathroom outside and gave me the key to unlock it.

I left the Old Black Lion for a stroll. The town was still sporting the bunting from the literary festival as well as posters in shop windows advertising the various events of the festival. I walked back to the road where I'd got off the bus. I was not sure if the bluff I had seen was part of the Black Mountains. I had trouble in recognizing this landscape as mountainous. It was covered with vegetation and there were trees at its summit, whereas the rugged peaks of the mountains, to my mind, should have been above the tree line.

The castle before me looked in need of repair. One or two windows on its upper floor were blocked by rusty sheets of iron. Another window was draped in a Union Jack. The precincts close by were quiet except for the occasional white vans driven by builders up and down its narrow roads. Two American women with cameras slung around their necks were looking in shop windows. I decided to take a walk along a country road leading out of the town. The road sloped down from a clock tower.

I found a takeaway food shop among the bookshops in this road. The man who ran it was friendly. People who came into his shop spoke to him about various local issues before ordering a meal. After eating at a table outside the shop, I carried on my walk. There was a builders' yard further down this road and perhaps that was why I had seen so many white vans driving in and out of town. There was also a supermarket nearby that was open till late. A small cottage housed a children's bookshop. The footpath ended further up this road and since it was quiet I decided to walk along its edge. The roaring of a tractor in a field could be heard at a distance. The road ahead became steep. I wanted to catch a glimpse of the town as it had been captured on a postcard I had seen. When I turned around, I realized that I was walking in the wrong direction and that the picture had probably been taken on the other side of the town. I returned to the Old Black Lion for an early night.

When I came down for breakfast the next morning, I found the men I had met the night before in the bar, now sitting at a table in one of the rooms. They were businessmen, staying in town for just a night. One of them greeted me. A black-uniformed waitress took their orders and then returned after a few minutes to take mine. The breakfast room had exposed timber beams. The dining facilities of this tavern had received an accolade from the Automobile Association displayed on the wall

I left the Old Black Lion soon after breakfast. It was a fine day and the town was getting ready for its trade in second-hand books, farm produce and furnishings. The empty spaces that I had seen the night before were now occupied by market traders, who had already set up their stalls. Some of them were selling bread, varieties of cheese and confectionery. A few of them were selling material for upholstery. There were also house plants for sale.

I wanted to say hello to the shopkeeper who also

owned a shop in London. I had found her shop when I arrived in the town the previous day. I went into the shop in the morning, expecting the lady I knew to be there, but there was no one at the counter. When I came back a few minutes later, I found a woman there. She had been making tea and emerged from a backroom with a cup in her hands. When I asked her about the owner of the shop, she told me she had gone to her other shop in London.

Some of the booksellers were stacking high the remainders and selling them at the uniform price of one or two pounds. Others, genre specialists, were sorting old books. One of the bookshops had a group of Americans as early customers. This small town, which has a bookshop for every forty residents, attracts a huge number of tourists every year. Otherwise, it would be impossible for so many bookshops to survive on local business alone. I came across many people in the morning who were visiting the town from other parts of Wales. It was the first time I'd heard the sound of Welsh. In fact, I confused the people who spoke it with Scandinavians. But when I heard a similar group of visitors speaking the same language, I realized my mistake.

I wanted to visit the bookshop in the castle first, as so much had been written about it and its owner. When I entered the shop, I saw a lady sitting behind a desk at the entrance. I left my bag with her just in case they didn't let people in who carried bags. I was the only customer in the shop – perhaps it was too early for the expected hordes.

Its collection of second-hand books was haphazard. There were far better second-hand bookshops in London, I thought. Not wanting to leave the castle empty-handed, I desperately searched for a book worth buying but failed to do so. I climbed down the stairs into the garden. The walls of the garden were lined with metal bookcases. Many books on these open shelves were damaged by rain and sun and sold for as little as twenty pence. This was the first time I'd seen a place in which books were exposed to the elements day and night.

After leaving the castle I found a coffee-shop with a couple of tables outside on the pavement. I went downstairs to order a coffee. The manager was on the phone so I had to wait until he'd finished before ordering. I sat outside for a little while and then the sun felt too hot so again I went downstairs where it was cooler. A few of the locals in the coffee-shop, still recovering from the visit of thousands of people during the previous week, were debating the merits of having so many bookshops in the town. They also seemed to resent the fact that the town had become a meeting place for literary agents and scouts.

The book trade had certainly contributed to the prosperity of the town. Hay could easily have fallen into decline, like so many rural areas, without its trade in second-hand books blooming in the last quarter of a century. Other towns in different countries were now trying to follow Hay's example. People came here from all around the world to buy books. The owner of the castle, who also owned many bookshops in the town, described it as his Kingdom of Books. It was indeed an empire of the mind. It was astonishing that a small town at the border of England and Wale attracted so many visitors. I met a foreign publisher who told me that they translated many English titles into their language but UK publishers hardly translated any works published in their country.

I entered a few more bookshops before drifting towards Broad Street to see the River Wye flowing through the valley. I was surprised to see a sign for a library in the town where one could buy a book for as little as twenty pence. I was curious to find out how many people used this facility so I followed the sign towards the library but found its door shut: closed for lunch. I decided to come back and ask the librarian if they had a copy of a mock documentary on the town. Many shop windows in Hay carried advertisements stating that the documentary was being shown at 'the Globe'. I had asked one or two booksellers for directions to this place but they were unable to help. One of them asked me if it was an art gallery. Then I saw a postman on the road and asked him where the Globe was. He pointed to a big house across the road. An elderly man wearing a cowboy hat was tending its garden. I asked him if the documentary was being shown in the house. He told me that the house was closed and was open to the public only during the festival.

Walking down the hill, I found a road on the left

leading to a bridge, the length of which suggested that there was a river flowing under it. I had only seen a rivulet on the other side of the town. The River Wye was flowing swiftly under the bridge. A number of canoes in bold colours were approaching it. There were mostly children in them, guided by two or three adults.

The library had opened by the time I returned and there were already a few people sitting in the reading room. I asked one of the librarians if he had a DVD of the documentary I was looking for. They didn't have it, but he gave me the telephone number of the lady who had produced it. I tried her number and it went to voicemail. I didn't leave a message because I wanted to see if one of the bookshops sold it. I tried a few bookshops without luck. Then a bookseller told me that I should try the shop that sold electronic goods. He gave me its name, telling me that everybody in the town knew its owner.

The shop was located in a side street. It was so small that I had gone past it without noticing it. The shopkeeper said he didn't stock DVDs and told me to try the music shop in town. I had seen this music shop but thought it unlikely they would have a copy of the documentary. As it turned out, they did have a few copies. When I asked the shop assistant if he had sold any he said they'd sold two or three copies during the festival.

I was feeling hungry and went into a nearby sandwich shop that looked newly built. One of the customers had ordered a sandwich a while ago and the teenager who had taken his order had forgotten about it. The customer was complaining about the service but the staff took no notice. I ordered a cheese and tomato sandwich, expecting it to take some time, but it arrived quite promptly – a badly made sandwich with too much grated cheese. The price of the sandwich was slightly higher than one would pay in London.

I left the sandwich shop to visit an information centre nearby. I asked the lady at the information desk how far was Hay Bluff. Assuming I was a motorist, she told me I could drive up there. She asked me where in London I lived and then told me that her daughter was living in London in Palmers Green. I asked her if the car park in the town was big enough for so many visitors during the festival. She replied that a temporary car parking facility was provided for them.

When I left the information centre, I bumped into someone I'd got to know in London many years ago. James, who lived a few doors down the road in my neighbourhood, aspired to be a novelist but worked in a bicycle shop. I remembered him having a French girlfriend who was very temperamental. He came from Toronto in Canada. His grandparents lived in Essex, but his parents had emigrated to Canada before he was born. I hadn't seen him for many years when he moved out of the neighbourhood. I was surprised to find him in Hay and asked him what had brought him there. He said that he'd decided to move to Hay six months ago in the hope of finding time to finish his novel.

I asked James about his girlfriend. He told me he had broken up with her soon after moving to a different neighbourhood in London. He had lived with two or three women since then and ended his relationship with his last girlfriend a few months before moving to Hay. He considered his relationships as one of the reasons why he'd been unable to finish his novel. He therefore aimed at living a solitary life in Hay for some time, working as a second-hand bookseller. He told me that it was a romantic idea for him to move to a book town and work as a bookseller in order to pursue his vocation. He earned very little as a second-hand bookseller but he hoped it would help him fulfil his wish to become a novelist.

I was interested to hear his impressions of Hay after living there for six months. James said that he'd found the town very friendly when he first moved there. But he came to realize that the locals didn't like the idea of people coming from elsewhere to live in Hay. They complained endlessly about prices in the town having gone up since people from London and other places had moved in. James said that it didn't matter to the locals if their town was visited by a well-known poet or a playwright. They didn't like it that the town had been taken over by the bookshops. They preferred to see more of the shops in town selling other things. The person who had started the book trade in Hay didn't like the people from London intervening in rural affairs. He had proclaimed himself the King of Hay in jest.

James was not sure how much more time he was going to spend in the town. How far he had got with his novel? He was only about halfway through. He'd been able to concentrate on his writing during the first three months and then followed other pursuits connected to living in the country. He had become a rambler and spent his weekends mostly tramping the countryside. I had seen a notice-board for ramblers in the town with a map of Wales showing tracks stretching as far as hundreds of miles. But James felt a bit uneasy lately, living among country folk who resented the idea of people coming from London to settle in the town.

He actually felt more at home in London than he felt in Toronto where he grew up. It was only the friends of his grandparents (themselves Londoners) who sometimes referred to him as someone "from the colonies". James had enjoyed living a bohemian life in London. His parents lived a middle-class life in Toronto, planning everything in advance. They were the kind of people who bought their Christmas cards at the beginning of the year, when they were cheaper and hoarded them for eleven months. They considered their son to be an idler.

I asked James whether working as a bookseller had given him any inspiration to work on his novel. He said that perhaps it wasn't such a good idea to work as a bookseller and aspire to be a novelist. He had found it dispiriting to sell second-hand books to people who were always price-conscious. Some of them were surprised to find an odd second-hand book selling for as much as two-thirds of its original price. Only a handful of people were prepared to buy a second-hand book at any price.

James told me that he had been trying to raise some money to spend on his writing project. I was curious to know how much money he needed to accomplish this task. He said that he'd be thrilled if he could raise a few hundred pounds in the next three months. He wanted to buy a computer to replace the electric typewriter he'd been using. This was the only tool of his trade, he said.

He had lived with a few other women since breaking up with his French girlfriend but felt that he was not getting anywhere entering into relationships one after another. James wanted to finish his novel before starting another relationship. He had met a woman in Hay who seemed very friendly. But he earned very little as a bookseller, even finding it difficult to afford an occasional bus fare to Hereford. He was wiser now and wanted to take his work seriously. He had met a few poets and novelists in the last few months who were not earning enough to support themselves even though a few of their books were still in print. He was therefore not too optimistic that his financial situation would improve dramatically even if he found a publisher for his work. He knew several writers doing odd jobs. Many people, he said, had this idea that writers become financially independent as soon as they get published. In fact, a writer's life is usually very tough. I asked James if he was prepared for such a life.

He replied that sometimes he wanted to give up the ghost and live a normal life.

James hadn't told his parents about his ambition to become a novelist. They wouldn't take him seriously, thinking that it was too late for him to start. His younger brother and sister were both raising families and had jobs which paid them well. They owned big houses in Toronto. His brother was ten years younger than him and had married a year ago. James hadn't gone to his brother's wedding. He said it would have been difficult for him to be there because his family regarded him as a failure. He didn't want middle-class people to look down on him.

What was it that made him move to Hay-on-Wye? He'd wanted to live for a while without the distractions of city life, he said. He had chosen to be without a television or a telephone. He kept in touch with his friends in London by using the local library internet facility. An active cyclist in London, James found that Hay was small enough to go everywhere on foot. Had moving to Hay helped him at all to get closer to achieving his ambition of becoming a novelist? He would have been better off, he now believed, taking up a day job in London and writing during the night. He had realized after living for a few months in Hay that the town offered very few possibilities. He also didn't like rural politics.

I spent some time in the afternoon with James after seeing him by chance outside the Hay-on-Wye information centre. Now I needed to catch the bus in time to get to

Hereford to board a train to London. On the way back home, having forgotten to bring my medication with me from London, I found I'd caught hay fever.

Birmingham Balti

The second biggest city in Britain attracts very few visitors from overseas. I was therefore surprised when an American visiting London told me that he wanted to go to Birmingham to see the industrial decline in the town. I had passed through Birmingham only once, on my way to another town in the Midlands, but felt no inclination to visit the city that was an hour and a half away from London by train. I could not find an excuse to go there.

One day I read in a newspaper that Birmingham had a sizable population of Kashmiri people living in one of the poorest districts in the country. But I had heard tales of their prosperity in Kashmir. In fact, they were people from Mirpur in Pakistan. Someone had told me that they sent all kinds of electrical appliances to their relatives in Mirpur. When I was desperately looking for work after my arrival in London, an Asian trader suggested that I go to Birmingham where many businesses were owned by Kashmiri people. But a few people from Srinagar whom I met in London didn't consider them Kashmiris because they didn't speak the same language. One of them told me that he had found the Mirpuris very different in character.

For some time, I assumed that Balti cuisine served in Indian restaurants in London came from Baltistan in the Korakaram Range. Then I discovered that it came from Birmingham instead. Whenever I leafed through the menus of Indian restaurants in London, I noticed that many dishes had been given Kashmiri names. But I was unfamiliar with those dishes. People who dined in Indian restaurants in London would sometimes tell me that they liked a certain Kashmiri dish cooked with fruit. I had never tasted a fruity dish in Kashmir. Why, then, did Bengali restaurateurs use Kashmiri names for their dishes? Could it be that these menus were first created in Birmingham by Mirpuri people? I therefore became curious to visit the place of birth of Balti cuisine.

I also wanted to see Zaffer, who had married a Mirpuri woman from Birmingham and moved there two years ago. He was a student at University College London when I knew him. He had fallen in love with a fellow student, Naseema, who was from the Small Heath area of Birmingham. Naseema's mother had objected to the idea of her daughter choosing her own husband, especially as Zaffer came from Hyderabad in India and Naseema's mother didn't like her son-in-law to be darker than her own people. Also Zaffer was lean and had the physique of a long distance runner, unlike many Mirpuris.

Naseema's mother had refused to meet Zaffer for many months but then was persuaded by other members of the family to see him. Zaffer was horrified when she asked him some insolent questions. For example, she wanted to know whether he owned the flat he occupied in London. In fact, Zaffer came from an educated background. His father was a High Court judge and his mother was a university lecturer. He had found it vulgar to be questioned by a woman from Mirpur. However, he was respectful in his conversation with her for the sake of her daughter, whom he loved.

In the end Naseema's family agreed to let her marry Zaffer. The wedding was to take place at a venue in Birmingham. Zaffer's parents came from Hyderabad to attend the wedding. He planned to travel with his father and a few friends to Birmingham and then bring the bride with him to London. Zaffer's mother wanted to stay in London to welcome the bride and groom home. But just one day before, Naseema's mother decided to call off the wedding. She could not hide her distress at her daughter marrying outside the Mirpuri community. However, that did not deter Naseema, who left home and took refuge in the house of one of her uncles, who wanted to see her happy. Zaffer had no idea about the goings-on in Small Heath until after he set out with his wedding party in a chauffeured car from London. When he was halfway between London and Birmingham, he received a phone call from Naseema's uncle asking him to wait for them in an Indian restaurant in Broad Street in Birmingham where he duly signed a marriage contract in the presence of an Imam. Zaffer was embarrassed in the company of his friends. But his father comforted him with a few kind words. Zaffer wanted his father to hide their unceremonious reception in Birmingham from his mother, who would have been heartbroken.

Naseema's mother died a few months later after a brief illness. Some people thought it was her daughter marrying someone she didn't approve of that killed her. Although Zaffer's mother-in-law had treated him with contempt, he decided to accompany his wife to her funeral. They stayed at the family house in Small Heath for a few days. Naseema's father asked her to come back to live with the family now that her mother had passed away. Zaffer thought that it was probably not a good idea for him to move in with Naseema's family but, for the sake of his wife, did not express his feelings.

A week later Zaffer and Naseema packed their few belongings in London and moved to Small Heath in Birmingham. Naseema's father owned a four-bedroom house in the area where most of the Mirpuris in Birmingham lived. Naseema had two elder sisters who were married to their cousins and lived nearby. She also had two younger brothers who lived in the same house. Naseema was the only woman in the household and therefore became responsible for most of the chores. She cooked food for everyone in the family.

Zaffer, who held a degree in Business Management from the University of London, tried to find a job in Birmingham but failed. He realized while living in Small Heath that without a job he was valued less as a member of his new family. At first, he didn't want to work for his father-in-law but without a job he was losing self-esteem with every passing day. Naseema's father owned a general store in the area so Zaffer eventually agreed to work for him.

The few people working in the general store were all related to Naseema's father. For instance, the shop was supervised by an elderly uncle of his. Zaffer found that he was not given any wages. It was an honorary kind of work for him to supervise the shop. He had no idea how much the other men were paid, those who worked there every day of the week. He felt like an extra among such a workforce. Zaffer had to forget the management theories he was taught at university and work within a Mirpuri tribal hierarchy in which he felt out of place. Some of them regarded him as an outsider. On top of this, Zaffer's parents were not happy for their son to live at his father-in-law's house. There was a derogatory name for such a man in Hyderabad.

A few months after moving to Birmingham, Naseema was expecting her first baby. So Zaffer had to hide his own misery from her and carry on working in his father-in-law's general store. He learned that the other men working in the shop had recently come from Mirpur to marry their cousins in Birmingham. Some of them had never been to another town in Britain. London was like a different country for them. They were fearful of travelling outside Birmingham, having found shelter among their relatives. Zaffer had good cause to regret leaving London for Birmingham, where his prospects seemed gloomy.

Naseema gave birth to a baby girl on their first wedding anniversary. Zaffer was happy that it was a girl, whereas Naseema's family would have liked the first-born to be a boy. Zaffer wanted to move out of his father-in-law's house soon after Naseema gave birth. He didn't want to continue working in a general store where his university degree was held in contempt. Zaffer thought it better to live in a garret elsewhere than a big house presided over by his father-in-law. He wanted to find another job but couldn't look for one while he was still living with Naseema's family. Naseema was conscious of her husband's predicament so she agreed to move out of her family home and live somewhere else in Birmingham. Zaffer would have liked to move back to London but reckoned that he wouldn't be able to rent a flat so long as he had no job. He found affordable accommodation in a high-rise building along a busy road in Birmingham. A few days later, he was lucky enough to find a job as a bank clerk.

I planned to stay in Birmingham for two days so I decided to take my bicycle with me. The train stopped at a couple of stations before reaching Birmingham International Station. I had always wondered why it was known as an international station when there were no trains departing from Birmingham to other countries. I realized when the train stopped at this station that its misleading name came from its nearness to Birmingham International Airport. The station also serves the National Exhibition Centre. A few minutes later the train reached New Street Station. Before the train pulled into the station I caught sight of a futuristic structure with a curved roof sporting aluminum disks like polka dots. I got lost in a subterranean level of the station trying to get my bicycle out by using the lifts.

It was sunny when the train left London, but it was cloudy on arrival in Birmingham. The overcast sky made the city look bleak. I found an information centre at a short distance from the station, went in to pick up a copy of the city map and asked the woman behind the counter if there was a bus tour of the city. There was not. Was there any kind of walking tour? She looked it up on her computer and said that the earliest was next week. I thought it better to ask her directions to my hotel instead. She told me that Holloway Circus, where the hotel was located, was just down the road.

When I had booked my accommodation there, I enquired about the distance of the hotel from the city centre.

The woman who made my reservation said that the hotel was only ten minutes away from the centre. Since I myself worked in the hotel industry, I thought that improbable and prepared to walk for twenty minutes.

I looked around Holloway Circus in vain for a signpost to the hotel. Having circled the roundabout twice, I cycled up Holly Head, stopping at a petrol station further up the road to ask directions. The man at the counter said that I should ask the taxi driver who was filling up outside. He was very friendly and gave me elaborate directions for a relatively short distance. The hotel was hidden in a side road and I had been looking for it along the main road. It was built like an American motel, with a car park in the forecourt enclosed by a wire mesh fence.

I pressed the buzzer and a receptionist let me in. After sorting out my room, I left the hotel and cycled back towards the city centre. I was the only cyclist on the road. I found that motorists in Birmingham, unlike those in London, were reluctant to overtake a cyclist. I also noticed on my way back to the centre that builders were constructing a pagoda-style fountain in the middle of Holloway Circus. Near the roundabout, a sleek high-rise building with an angular front was undergoing finishing touches. Next on view was a circular building known as The Rotunda. Its name evoked images of classical architecture but it was a shabby structure like the British Telecom tower in London.

I walked along an inclined pathway with my bike to reach New Street. Guarding the entrance of a shopping centre was a raging bull cast in bronze. This was Birmingham's famous shopping centre, known as The Bull Ring. I had heard that this shopping centre was going to be demolished. But then someone told me to my disappointment that it had already been rebuilt a few years ago. The concrete structure of the shopping centre was pulled down but the iron and steel Rotunda had survived. The residents of Birmingham had actually campaigned for it to be preserved as a listed building.

I caught sight of the spire of an old church behind the shopping centre. Looking at it from an elevated street level, it seemed as if the church had sunk into the ground. This prospect looked surreal because it's usually the case that a spire towers over a town.

I asked a newspaper vendor for directions to the Central Library. He said that I should carry on walking until the end of the street and then cross over to the other side of a square to find a precinct which had a McDonald's inside, and that was the location of the Central Library. When I reached Victoria Square, it offered fine examples of architecture around it. A sphinx-like animal carved in stone sat in front of a Renaissance-style building known as Council House. The Town Hall, modelled on the Roman Temple at Nîmes, was shrouded in plastic and undergoing restoration.

It was designed by Joseph Hansom, who was also the inventor of the hansom cab.

I heard the echo of an amplified voice coming from the rear of the Town Hall. When I turned the corner, I saw a giant television screen mounted on the scaffolding by Birmingham City Council to broadcast news to passers-by. There was a multi-tiered concrete structure on the other side, built like an upside-down pyramid. A McDonald's sign in this building's lobby confirmed that the Central Library was also within. There were many people walking through its doors. I climbed up a few floors on an escalator to find the section of the library that held books of local interest.

I left the library shortly afterwards, wanting to be somewhere less crowded. The classical building nearby, which housed a museum and an art gallery, offered me a place for retreat. But it was late afternoon and the building was due to close in half an hour so I decided to come back in the morning. I walked back to the other end of New Street to pick up my bicycle. The street was full of office workers heading towards the train station to go home.

I wanted to see Ladypool Road in the Small Heath area where Zaffer had worked for his father-in-law. I had read in a brochure that the area was also known as the Balti Triangle and was being marketed everywhere. Large banners bearing 'Be in Birmingham' slogans hung from high-rise buildings. It seemed as if the city was being marketed as a destination for people living in smaller towns in the Midlands.

I cycled downhill to Holloway Circus and then uphill towards Five Ways to get to Small Heath. I would have liked to take the back roads but wasn't sure if I had a choice. I had to cycle along the Ring Road used by lorries and coaches. There were many tower-blocks along this road, some of them quite recently built. I wondered what kind of people chose to live in these tower-blocks. Then I saw an indoor shopping complex nearby. Perhaps one of the attractions for them was quick access to a motorway and another was these shopping complexes surrounded by car parks. A white dome and minaret was visible in the distance and I knew I was travelling in the right direction. It was Birmingham's Central Mosque, built halfway between Small Heath and the city centre along Ring Road.

I turned into Highgate Road, which cuts through the Balti Triangle. A few Asian boys were playing cricket in a small park, using plastic crates for stumps. When I reached Ladypool Road, I saw a few derelict buildings at a corner. The traffic light was reclining on the ground. I had to look out for cars before turning into Ladypool Road. There were more Indian restaurants than shops along this road. A minibus pulled in to one side of the road and dropped a group of women who had come to dine in one of the restaurants there.

Grocers were selling a wide variety of fruit and vegetables on display outside their shops. The men who worked there wore green coats and the shoppers were mostly wearing long shirts and loose trousers. One of the bigger premises was doing a brisk business selling baby products such as pushchairs. There must have been a baby boom in the Small Heath area of Birmingham and someone had the foresight to open this business among the restaurants. Further down the road, I was surprised to see a marriage bureau operating from a room above the shops. I had assumed that most of the marriages around here were arranged privately without the need for such a service.

I drifted into other streets which formed the sides of the Balti Triangle, to discover shops selling Indian sweets, dried fruit and jewellery. There were also a few textile shops selling fabrics. It reminded me of similar shops in Srinagar. One day someone told me that those shops in my home town were going to disappear in the near future and all the clothes would be made in factories. I was thrilled to hear this prediction, without realizing it had already happened in Europe and America. Our tailors in Srinagar never kept their promises. They would tell their loyal customers that clothes were going to be ready on a certain date only to give them another date on the appointed day. Sometimes they would repeat this procedure for months before fulfilling their promise. Occasionally they would set up a temporary workshop in a client's home if there was a wedding in the family and the father of the groom ordered clothes to be made for everyone.

I wanted to taste the Birmingham Balti now that I was inside the triangle, but it was difficult to pick a restaurant among the numerous Balti houses in the neighbourhood. It had made me smile when I heard that Balti was the name of a frying pan and not a region in the Karakoram mountains. Just one restaurant in Ladypool Road described its cuisine as Mirpuri. I wasn't sure if the restaurant owner was being honest or if it was a marketing ploy. I was looking for a café-style restaurant where one orders food at the counter. It was early in the evening and most of the restaurants were empty, but I found it difficult to walk inside and ask for a table for one. I walked up and down the road twice, trying to find a place that was less formal. I found one or two café-style restaurants but they didn't look very inviting. In one of the restaurants I saw a diner sitting by a window gnashing chicken bones, and walked past it very quickly. Waiters in white starched uniforms stood by the door of another restaurant. Yet another had a baroque interior and was run by a Sikh family.

The air in Ladypool Road had an odour of Balti food. I was getting hungry and finally decided to eat in a restaurant in which food was laid out in chrome dishes and diners helped themselves. There were only a few people in the restaurant when I came in but it soon began to fill up. Some of the diners were carrying their own drinks with them. A few were carrying multiple packs of beer. The price of the buffet was very reasonable. Most of the diners were filling their plates with generous portions of Balti food and all of them were going for a second helping after washing down the first with beer. The restaurant in Ladypool Road seemed to be popular with English people, many of whom had become experts in eating Indian food with their hands. I found the food a bit too hot for my taste buds and tried a small portion of halva to soothe my mouth after the meal.

I felt heavy when I left the restaurant and was glad that I was cycling for a few miles back to my hotel. I wanted to follow the same route towards the city centre. However, I went past a roundabout and then turned into Broad Street. It was lively at night. There were many trendy restaurants in Broad Street, some of them also serving Balti food. The doorman of a pub along this road was wearing Pathan-style white trousers and a long black coat. There were a few big hotels further up this road. I cycled as far as a Ferris wheel and then turned back towards the roundabout and finally found my way to the hotel.

I had heard about the Jewellery Quarter in Birmingham long before visiting the town. I wanted to visit its museum and left the hotel at nine the next morning to go there. I had seen a sign near Victoria Square pointing towards the Jewellery Quarter the day before. I passed a fine terracotta building after the square, cycled down Constitution Hill and then asked a postman for directions. He told me to turn left into one of the side roads and then look for a clock tower, which would lead me into the Jewellery Quarter.

There was a Sikh temple at the top of the road. I passed the clock tower and then found an information centre near a multi-storey building. I went inside the centre to ask for information but the desk was unmanned. I waited for a few minutes but no one appeared so I left. I had thought of the Jewellery Quarter as a part of town full of grand architecture befitting its trade in precious metal. But I was disconcerted to see the run-down buildings in the neighbourhood. One of the derelict buildings had wild plants growing on its ledges. I was unsure if this was actually the Jewellery Quarter until I saw the sign outside the station that bore its name.

The windows of the small brick building in the Quarter were fitted with shutters behind which were showcases displaying necklaces and rings made of gold and silver. Some of these windows had plastic awnings above them. Many workshops had gaudy signs fitted on their exteriors. I found the museum but it was closed. When I pressed the buzzer, someone opened the door and told me that the museum would open after an hour and a half, at 11:30 am. I decided to cycle back to Chamberlain Square and spend a few hours in Birmingham Museum & Art Gallery instead.

On my way back, I passed The Pen Room, belonging to the Birmingham Pen Trade Heritage Association. Until the 1950s, when ballpoint pens came into use, the vast majority of pen nibs used all over the world were made in Birmingham. At one time, the factories producing pen nibs in Birmingham employed 5000 men and women. The nibs were handmade before being mass-produced in the factories around the Jewellery Quarter. Their dominance of the world market lasted over a hundred years. Then the Hungarian inventor, Laszlo Biro, made the first ballpoint pen and its popularity spread all over the world.

A marble stairway at the entrance of the museum in Chamberlain Square led me to a circular room in its Art Gallery. I wanted to see the Museum first but got distracted by the works of the Pre-Raphaelites, a group of artists who returned to a style of painting that was popular before the Renaissance. They had won the support of John Ruskin. I had seen a plaque on the exterior of a building in Bloomsbury in London where this group was formed in the middle of the nineteenth century. But I was unfamiliar with the works of the group members except for Gabriel Dante Rossetti. I got drawn into the other rooms of the Art Gallery until I forgot about the Museum.

I looked at Ford Madox Brown's *The Last of England* and then returned to the round room en route for the Industrial Gallery of the Museum. It was in an adjacent space but I hadn't noticed it on my way in. It displayed ceramics and glass objects. I was hoping to see other industrial age products in this room. I was intrigued by the contrivances fitted on the ceiling of the Industrial Gallery. It was only later that I realized they were gas lamps

Wanting to sit down for a few minutes before visiting the other section of the Museum, I found the entrance of the Edwardian Tea Room at the far end of the Industrial Gallery. It was peaceful to sit there under the gaze of the great masterpieces on its walls. Then I went to an upper floor to see an exhibition called *Visions of Birmingham*. I had already seen the futuristic design of Richard Rogers for the new library. It was like replacing one monstrosity with another. The model of a grand plan for the centre of Birmingham was on display. So far only one of the buildings in the model had been erected. It was hard to guess how long it would take to erect the rest of the buildings in the plan. When I saw a Mirpuri family taking a leisurely walk through the gallery, it reminded me that I was to meet Zaffer that evening.

I had already spent a good part of the day here and I had no desire to go back to the Jewellery Quarter to see its museum. I was about to leave when I saw a sign for a room displaying goods manufactured in Birmingham. On display in this gallery was a wide variety of buttons, both pearl and brass. Birmingham was once the centre of button manufacturing in the world. The town had also supplied buttons for soldiers' uniforms during the American Civil War. The processes used in button making were later adapted to produce pen nibs. It seems ludicrous now that Birmingham's industrial strength came from manufacturing such small products. I wandered around the gallery thinking how Britain had conquered the world in the nineteenth century by the export of pen nibs and buttons. I also found old-style weighing scales on display made by Avery. Such scales are still in use in India today.

That evening I met Zaffer in the same coffee-shop in New Street where I had stopped in the morning. He had finished his day's work. I wanted to know what he thought of Birmingham, having lived there for two years. Zaffer said that he had found the town uninspiring after moving there from London. He also felt let down by Naseema's family. What about various regeneration projects taking place in Birmingham to reverse the industrial decline? Zaffer said he preferred London as a city where there are many parks and gardens. He had found Birmingham, in contrast, a city of roundabouts and multi-storey car parks. Zaffer hadn't liked the idea of owning a car in London. However, it had seemed a necessity for him to drive one in Birmingham. He didn't like the drudgery of working in a bank but he had accepted this job because he wanted to get out of Small Heath. He was trying for a transfer to London where the bank he worked for had many branches.

I wanted Zaffer to accompany me to the International Conference Centre in Broad Street, which I'd seen from the outside the night before. The ICC was one of the city's regeneration projects. A Ferris wheel, the one I'd seen the day before, was spinning gently with a few people on board in front of the centre. The building, which also housed the Birmingham Symphony Orchestra, looked like an airport terminal from the inside – a disconcerting location for a symphony hall. I saw a poster of a forthcoming concert of a master musician from the Indian subcontinent. Thinking the tickets for the concert would have been sold out in view of the large number of Asians living in Birmingham, I went to the ticket counter and asked out of curiosity if there were any tickets left. The man behind the counter told me plenty of seats were available.

I asked Zaffer about the 'Be in Birmingham' campaign. He told me that the project was partly funded by the European Regional Development Fund. Zaffer wanted to show me a nearby square called Brindley Place. We left the ICC from the canal side entrance and crossed over a bridge to reach it. There was a pub on the other side of the canal and a couple of boats were moored to the bank. The pub had a few tables outside on the pavement. I remembered seeing its picture in a promotional brochure seeking to sell the retro look of this pub. Brindley Place looked neat and was surrounded by stylish buildings. There were many fountains in the square gushing forth white columns of water. A coffee-shop housed in a moth-like glass structure was located in the middle of the square. Perhaps it was the precursor of the new design for the Central Library. On our way back, we passed a multi-storey car park. I had associated the city with car-manufacturing plants rather than car parks and roundabouts.

I asked Zaffer where he was planning to live in London if he got transferred there. A place in East or West London was what he was looking for. He had lived in Central London as a student but thought it would be too expensive for him to find accommodation there. Zaffer wanted to sell his car before moving to London and rely on public transport. It would give him pleasure, he said, to be back among the friends he had made in London.

We walked up to New Street where Zaffer bade me farewell. I picked up my bicycle, feeling glad that I'd brought it with me to Birmingham. It had given me freedom of movement. I felt sympathy for Zaffer and hoped that he would get transferred to London soon where I could catch up with him again.

Palm Trees in Bournemouth

It was my first journey out of London since the July bombings. I hadn't boarded a train in London for several weeks. When I cycled to Central London as usual in the afternoon of 7th July, I saw a tide of people walking in the opposite direction. I had never seen Mornington Crescent as a pedestrian thoroughfare until then. I cycled as far as Euston Road and then decided to turn back because I didn't want to see a deserted town. The return journey gave me some idea how many people used the Underground every day. A few days later, I heard from a bicycle shop owner that the demand for bicycles had gone up. I was terrified to think that the thousands of people I had seen walking to their homes a few days before might decide to cycle to work. It brought to mind the nightmarish scene of an oriental city. I thought it was a dangerous idea to encourage so many commuters to ride bicycles. A few days later, I saw the Transport for London adverts urging people to ride bicycles that might be rusting in the back gardens of their homes. A few weeks later, I heard on the news that it was in fact dangerous to ride a bike in

London. It was a relief to know that the vast majority of people who used the Underground wouldn't surge overground.

Commuters went back to using the Underground but tourists were hesitant for some time. A Californian couple told me they were prepared to walk a few miles rather than use the Underground. The first thing I had noticed when I arrived in London from the Continent was the absence of rubbish bins at train stations. It took me some time to realize that the IRA had been active in the city for some time and that rubbish bins could serve as bomb repositories.

I crossed Waterloo Bridge to reach the train station – the first time I was to board a train from there. It was a fine day in London and I had to persuade myself to take the trouble of making a trip to Bournemouth. I had arranged to meet Kumara there. Otherwise I would have gone another day. After the July bombings, someone I knew who lived in Dorset had compared London with Srinagar. I thought the comparison was absurd.

I had met Kumara a year ago in London when he worked as a carer. He was from Colombo in Sri Lanka. His friend, Ragu, had told me that Kumara was a doctor by training but he had run away from home after creating hostility between two communities there. Kumara, whose parents were Buddhists, had fallen in love with Meena, a Muslim woman. He wanted to convert to Islam in order to marry his beloved and be accepted by her family. He had consulted one or two mullahs who asked him his motive for changing his religion. He told them the truth and they had found it unacceptable. Perhaps they could foresee the wrath of the majority if this news became public. However, the gossip about Kumara and his longing for a Muslim girl had spread fast. Both of them received threats that they should stop seeing each other. Kumara left the country in the hope that one day Meena would join him.

I first saw Kumara in a London park pushing an elderly patient in a wheelchair. Ragu had told me about him. Kumara was afraid that he could become a target of a Sri Lankan gang in London. He had seen Sri Lankan men living in London getting into fights over women. He was an eyewitness to one of these fights when Ragu had taken him to a party. He was recognised there by someone who had recently come from Sri Lanka. It was a small world when it came to Sri Lankans living in London. Most of the men worked at petrol stations and the gossip spread from one petrol station to another very quickly. Kumara was Singhalese whereas Ragu and all his friends were Tamils.

Kumara had heard people talking about his predicament. He feared that he could get beaten up any time by a gang so he wanted to leave London and go into hiding somewhere else. Ragu had supported him for the first few months when he had arrived from Colombo without any belongings except for sad memories of his romance with a woman of another faith. He felt desperately lonely. His friends in Colombo had predicted that he would soon overcome his grief when he found another woman. They were wrong. There was a dearth of Sri Lankan women in London. There were far more Sri Lankan men than women in the town, which caused many fights whenever they got together. At one big party Kumara saw hundreds of men and only a dozen women.

One day, thinking it might lessen his grief, Ragu's friends took Kumara to a brothel in East London that they frequented. He was surprised to see them spending their money there, men who worked from dawn to dusk in the petrol stations, emanating petrol fumes just as those who worked in Indian restaurants in London smelt of curry. But these were men without women and he didn't condemn them for their weekly excursions. Some of them worked in the petrol stations for years on end without a break.

Waterloo Station was busy with people travelling to various destinations south of London and those going to Paris by Eurostar. An announcement reminded us of the heightened security situation. But most of the passengers seemed to be relaxed. They must have heard this announcement over and over during the last few weeks.

Since Kumara had told me that the town centre was about twenty minutes walking distance from the train station, I decided to take my bicycle with me. A kindly train driver helped me store it in a small bike compartment. The train glided through the unfamiliar landscape of South London towards Weymouth. We passed Southampton, from where many wealthy people took their luxury cruises to New York and various Mediterranean ports. The landscape looked marshy, with one or two ships in view. A few people got off the train here and a few more boarded it to go to Bournemouth.

It was sunny when I arrived in Bournemouth. I wanted to catch a glimpse of the seafront before going to the town centre to meet Kumara. I looked in vain for a sign to the seafront and then asked someone near a roundabout for directions. He told me he didn't know how to get there because he always took a bus. I decided to take one of the roads branching from the roundabout. At the end of the road I was surprised to find myself at the top of a cliff. A few men and women were sitting on the benches on the cliff enjoying the sun. They were elderly, neatly dressed, and looked very calm. A short distance from the cliff top was a large block of flats overlooking the sea. I wondered whether the people sitting on the benches lived in those desolate flats.

There was a lift taking people down from the cliff. The beach below the cliff was crowded with people sunbathing and playing ball games. At the top of the cliff one could hear a distant buzz from the vast number of people on the beach. Perhaps that was why the older folk had chosen to sit on the benches on the cliff. I asked one of them for directions to the hotel where I was booked in for the night. They told me that the hotel was located on the other cliff on the west side of the pier. I wanted to see the hotel before going to the town centre where I was to meet Kumara in a coffee-shop called the Obscura Café. Its name struck me as odd, something which characterized Kumara's life in both London and Bournemouth.

I cycled downhill, reaching the road which led to the pier, and then along a steep road towards the West Cliff. I passed the Exeter Hotel, the first one to be built when the town was founded in the nineteenth century. There were rows of hotels on both sides of this road. The town felt touristy along West Cliff Road. I found my hotel further up. A redbrick Victorian building, its interior seemed to have changed little since that era. The Reception desk had old-style pigeonholes on the wall for keys and messages. I was allocated a room on the top floor.

It was a small room like the one I'd been given in Hay-on-Wye. After checking in, I left to meet Kumara and found the Obscura Café in the middle of a square with ease. The roof was built in the shape of a lantern. I looked without success for a hidden camera obscura that would have justified its name. Kumara was sitting at a table outside the coffee-shop. In the park across the square palm trees could be seen, seemingly shrunken by the temperate climate. I asked Kumara about the palm trees in Sri Lanka. He said they were very much taller. People who live in a temperate climate are fonder of tropical landscapes, just as those living in the tropics are attracted by temperate landscapes.

Nearby, a group of Arab students were playing a ball game. Kumara told me there were many language schools in the town that attracted students from various countries. He had himself thought of joining one after finding to his dismay that people understood him, if at all, with great difficulty. But he couldn't afford to pay the fees. I wanted to know more about his life in an English seaside town. And what about the few Sri Lankan families I'd seen there? Kumara said they were second generation Sri Lankans, visiting the town with small children from other parts of the country. He was not afraid of these people. But he was afraid of seeing any Sri Lankans from London. They usually drove down to Bournemouth in groups of five or six. He was surprised to see them driving big cars when many of them needed two jobs to survive.

I asked Kumara if he had heard from Meena since he had left Sri Lanka. Someone had told him that her parents had married her to an older man, a landowner. This man owned a few hectares of land with trees that yielded him a produce of coconuts five or six times a year. The man was a widower but Meena's parents didn't mind that because they thought it would have been difficult to find a match for her once everyone knew about her and Kumara.

I asked Kumara if he would accept her if she ever came back to him. He said that he would always welcome her with open arms, even if she was carrying another man's child.

Their own relationship had not been consummated. He had even thought of getting circumcised in order to marry her. Kumara said that he knew one or two Muslim men in Sri Lanka who had married European women of the Christian faith. A mullah had proclaimed them man and wife, thinking that one day these women would convert to the faith of their husbands.

There was a funfair in the park and a generally festive atmosphere. Kumara told me that he'd found this atmosphere in the town since he had arrived there a few months ago. It had made his life in Bournemouth bearable. What about the people walking in the park? Kumara said that the path led to the pier and many people were returning home from the beach. He thought the beach would be less busy now that it was six o'clock. I asked him to accompany me to the pier. The garden beyond the palm trees had African daisies and marigolds, which reminded me of the Pundits in Kashmir who used these flowers for worship in the temples, hence referred to as 'flowers of Pundits' in Srinagar.

A few people were playing golf on a miniature course in the park. There was an elaborate bandstand with a few rows of empty chairs in front of it. A sign informed visitors that we were in Hardy country – a Scottish lady in London used to tell me that he was a 'very English' writer. In fact, Kumara's life resembled a character in a Thomas Hardy novel, whose love of a woman doesn't diminish even after she weds another man.

The crowd I had seen earlier on the beach had dispersed. A few cleaners were picking up empty plastic bottles on the beach. A long-bearded man wearing headphones was looking for precious metal in the sand using a metal-detector. The hot day had ended in a hazy evening. Kumara told me that one could see as far as the Isle of Wight from the pier on a clear day.

We bought tickets for the pier since it was less frantic now. Kumara also wanted to say hello to his friend, Kriztof, who worked in a cafeteria on the pier. Kriztof came from Gdansk in Poland and had come to live in Bournemouth at the same time as Kumara. He was a cheerful person who refused to take payment for a drink from Kumara. We sat outside on a picnic table watching the setting sun painting the horizon with its hues. Kumara said that he came to the pier every evening. The ticket counter attendants recognised him as a regular and would sometimes let him in for free.

Curious about what kind of job he had found after giving up being a carer in London, I asked Kumara about his work in Bournemouth. It turned out that he was working as a nurse in a private hospital where people came from other countries for surgery. They preferred Bournemouth as a seaside town where they liked to convalesce after an operation. It was a better job, Kumara said, than being a carer in London. He had worked with an older Sri Lankan man in London who had been a carer for more than twenty-five years and had become as old-fashioned and grumpy as his patients.

He always wore a trilby hat and, thanks to the fetid environment he worked in, he smelled of chloroform. He was also curious about everyone else's salary. Kumara disliked the Sri Lankan owners of this nursing home in London. Although they were certainly wealthy they lived liked paupers.

Kumara had finished his degree with poor results. He had lost time in his love affair with Meena. His friends had gone to America and were working as doctors. Sometimes he wished he had gone there. I asked him about his prospects of working for the NHS. He said it would take a few years for him to qualify for an NHS job. He didn't have money to pay for taking the necessary exams and then registering himself with the British Medical Council. Besides, it was getting tougher for someone from overseas to find a job as a doctor in Britain. It didn't bother him much that he was working as a nurse. The real loss he felt was that of Meena. Nothing else really mattered to him.

How long did he plan on living in Bournemouth? He wasn't too sure. He had arrived there in spring and enjoyed the summer but he dreaded the winter. He wasn't used to the cold climate. During the last few months, he had always found something going on in the town. Although Kumara didn't take part, he liked the bustle of it all.

I wanted to know if the passing of time was healing his wounds. Kumara replied that he had found it difficult to forget about his misery. He hadn't made contact with his family since leaving Sri Lanka. His father had foreseen the trouble and considered him foolish to give up everything for the sake of a woman. Kumara's father was known among his kinsfolk for his wisdom and people hadn't expected such folly from his son. Kumara had severed contact with his mother to avoid hearing the taunts of his father through her.

The lights hanging like bunting around the pier shone brighter as the evening darkened. There were fewer people left on the pier as we walked towards the exit. We carried on walking through the park towards the place we had started from. I found my bicycle, locked in a rack near the square. A group of entertainers had gathered in the park. They were spinning ropes which glowed in the dark. Two German girls walking ahead of us were greeted by a group of Arab students. The girls mocked them by mimicking their "Hallos".

I said goodbye to Kumara and then cycled toward West Cliff through the town. The night air was very refreshing. But when I entered my hotel room it was stuffy. I wanted to open the windows to get some fresh air but they were fitted with another set of windows that slid to one side so I could only keep one side open. I had found a similar ingenuity of design in another hotel in London. It seemed that someone had come up with the idea of double windows instead of double-glazing. I wanted to leave the hotel and go back to the pier but Kumara had told me that it closed at 11 pm. The small room didn't cool off and the heat kept me awake until the early hours of the morning.

I got up a bit late, having finally fallen asleep at 4 am. The receptionist had told me the night before that breakfast was served until 9:30 am. The breakfast room was full of hotel residents by the time I joined them at 9:00. A 'full English breakfast' was laid out on a buffet table. The hotel guests were filling their plates with baked beans, omelettes and sausages. It was a gluttonous scene. I sat in a corner with some cereal and juice. The sizzling breakfast had raised the temperature of the room and the fans on the high ceiling were stirring the air gently. Wanting to breathe the fresh air outside the building, I did not linger in the breakfast room.

I intended to take a stroll on the promenade before it became crowded so I checked out of the hotel while many of the residents were still at their breakfast. I had seen a beach artist the day before, working dextrously with sand on statues of classical design. It was an impressive display and it was heartening to see the statues intact in the morning. It had been a dry night. I thought it admirable that this artist was working purely for the moment, unconcerned about posterity.

The rows of beach huts that look so colourful in pictures of English seaside towns were weathered, and many of them needed a fresh coat of paint. A few of these huts had 'For Hire' signs hanging on their doors. An elderly couple were laying a small table for breakfast in one of the huts and boiling a kettle on a gas stove. The sand on the beach was khaki-coloured. I had seen many people lying on it reading popular paperbacks. Perhaps these were titles that the Sunday newspapers recommended as 'Holiday Reading'. I wondered whether these paperbacks survived the elements or if their owners disposed of them before going home.

Since the promenade was starting to get crowded, I reckoned it was time for me to visit the other side of town. Kumara had recommended taking an open-top bus. I wasn't sure if Bournemouth was big enough for a bus tour. But the ticket-seller told me that the tour lasted for almost an hour and convinced me it was worth buying a ticket. In fact, the bus followed a route to another pier at Boscombe. I got on the bus near the pier at Bournemouth. Sitting on the upper deck, I heard a loud mechanical voice introducing the tour. I looked for speakers fitted onto the sides of the bus but couldn't find any. Then I found a megaphone-shaped speaker hidden under one of the seats.

The bus drove up the steep road towards West Cliff Road. There were many pine trees along the road, which gave the air a forest-like freshness. However, the shape of these pine trees was unusual. Some of them were slanting and the branches of others were spread out. The pine trees I knew were those of the upright Himalayan kind, which are very tall. Then someone on the bus told me that the pine was not native to Bournemouth but had been imported from Scotland over a hundred years ago. The wind had moulded these trees into bizarre shapes.

The bus passed through one or two places that offered

a fine view of the shimmering sea with its array of white sails. As the bus gained height the gorges with ravines, known as *chines* in Dorset, became deeper. A few place-names ended in 'Chine' along West Cliff. The bus made a loop to return to Exeter Road and then drove through the town towards Boscombe Pier. There were fewer people on this pier compared to the one in Bournemouth.

We passed a row of hotels facing the sea along Overcliff Drive. Bournemouth appeared more prosperous than many other English seaside towns. Some of the houses in the town were holiday homes. Founded two centuries ago, the town had prospered in the early 20th century because of people visiting for beach holidays and eventually it became popular as a retirement town. Even though many English people went abroad for beach holidays after the 1970s Bournemouth hadn't gone into decline. It still attracted people from other parts of Britain and from abroad.

I got off the bus near the Bournemouth Pier, where the tour had started. The beach was again full of sunbathers. Some of them were hiring kayaks to venture into the sea. Queues of people were waiting at the counter of a fish and chips shop near the promenade. Thinking the shop was busy because it sold fresh fish, I joined the queue and waited for my turn. The chips were tasty but the fish didn't seem so fresh. Evidently that didn't matter. It seemed it was simply a tradition to buy fish and chips on the promenade.

Before leaving Bournemouth I wanted to say goodbye

to Kumara, who didn't finish work until four o'clock, so I still had a few hours to wander around. Luckily, I saw a sign for a museum and followed it until I reached the entrance of what looked like a villa. It was the house of Merton Russell-Cotes, an ex-Mayor of the town who had bequeathed it to the nation. Its garden displayed various statues. Although it was not far from the beach it was hidden away from the main thoroughfare. A small reception area led me to a staircase and I found myself in a room full of Japanese artefacts. Also in this room was an exhibition of paintings by artists who had worked in Bournemouth and captured its seascape on their canvases. When I drifted into the dining room, its stained glass revealed Russell-Cotes' imperialist leanings. The panes in the bay window represented countries of the British Empire – Ceylon, Australia, Gibraltar and Malta. I found such relics of the empire in every town I had visited in the British Isles. There was also a wine cooler in the dining room that had been used by Napoleon when in exile on the island of St. Helena. The wall clock had 'Lund & Blockley (To The Queen) 42 Pall Mall' printed on its dial.

As I entered the main hall, I caught a glimpse of the frieze at the top of the stairwell, a reproduction in plaster of the Parthenon. This was the second time I had seen a replica of the Elgin Marbles – I had seen one in Nashville, Tennessee, many years ago. There were some very interesting paintings in the gallery. I was astounded to see *The Moorish Proselytes of Archbishop Ximenes* by Edwin Long, in which the Archbishop is depicted baptising Arabs in Granada. There was also a fine painting by Bevan Hay based on the biblical story of The Prodigal's Return. In another gallery, Bernard Shaw, cast in metal, held his head in his hands in apparent exasperation.

I went upstairs to have a look at rooms which had been given different names based on the colours of the spectrum. One of the upstairs rooms was dedicated to the tragedian actor, Henry Irving. Also on this floor was a Moorish Alcove based upon the designs of the Alhambra in Spain. A statue of a Moor was draped in real white cloth headgear. One of the arches of the alcove led to a boudoir. In the Victorian home, the boudoir (if it wasn't the bedroom itself) was usually situated close to the bedroom of the lady of the house. It would express her own taste and provide her with a place of retreat. The word 'boudoir' comes from the French verb *bouder*, to sulk – what was expected of a lady of leisure in Victorian times. I had also seen a drawing room downstairs. I often wondered in my childhood about the purpose of such a room in a mansion until I learnt it was actually the 'withdrawing room' used by women as a place of retreat after dinner. There was a glass screen in the boudoir with a selection of dead butterflies sealed inside it. They had lost their varied colours and turned sepia over the years.

It was already four o'clock when I next looked at my watch. I had spent a couple of hours in the museum and it was time now for me to say goodbye to Kumara. When I reached the pier, he was already there with Kriztof, who was not working that afternoon. We walked along the promenade past the beach huts to the far side. I was glad that Kumara had found a friend in Bournemouth. I asked them if they were planning a daytrip to London. Kriztof said he went to London now and again. Kumara hadn't seen his friend Ragu for a few months. I asked them to let me know beforehand about any visit they planned, then said goodbye to them both and cycled towards the train station. The train to London was not too crowded even though it was peak hour. Perhaps many Londoners visited Bournemouth by car. I had seen an unbroken line of cars trying to leave the town on my way to the station and felt relieved that I was travelling by train.

A few days later I saw the Sri Lankan man with whom Kumara worked with as a carer in London. He was walking through a park, unaccompanied this time by his wheelchair-bound patients. Although it was warm he was still wearing a trilby hat. I noticed his clothes were unusually grubby and he looked sullen. I wondered if he felt depressed after caring for elderly people for so many years. All in all, I thought Kumara had made the right decision in giving up his carer job in London to be a nurse in Bournemouth.

Made in Sheffield

Staying in a houseboat once in Srinagar, I was given a tour of the dining room by its owner to show off the memorabilia he had collected since the end of the Raj. In a well-rehearsed manner, he pulled open the drawer of a wooden chest to show me the markings on a set of cutlery. The knives and forks had 'Made in Sheffield' etched on them. My host told me the set once belonged to a certain titled Englishman who had stayed in his houseboat a few times and liked to use fine cutlery. The houseboat owner didn't let other guests use this set. I had heard about the tradition of people bringing their own cutlery to feasts in seventeenth-century England, but I was puzzled to see it being practised in the twentieth century. My host said that he had been to England two or three times and had even dined once at the stately home of his patron.

I wanted to visit Sheffield after I moved to London but found no reason to go there for many years. Then one day I met Zeinab. She was born in Aden in the mid-1960s and had moved to Sheffield with her parents in the 1970s. She held a degree from the School of African and Oriental Studies (SOAS) in London and worked for a voluntary organisation in Sheffield. I asked her how many Yemeni people lived there. It was difficult to tell the exact number but she thought their population was around five thousand. Many of them had moved there when Aden was still a British Crown colony and they worked mainly in the steel industry. The Yemenis who went to America had found work in factories in Detroit.

I could only guess Zeinab's age – it would have been impolite to ask her such a question – but she appeared to be in her late thirties. When I met her in London she wore dark glasses in the evening. Eventually I noticed that she was blind in one eye.

She told me about her voluntary work in Sheffield. Zeinab travelled to Yemen only occasionally. The last time she had been there was to attend the marriage of her younger sister. Her mother lived with her in Sheffield and her father had died ten years ago.

Zeinab was analytical about the challenges Yemenis faced while living in Sheffield. I asked her what it was like to go to Sana'a or Aden every few years. She said it was her responsiblity as a voluntary worker to give advice to Yemeni men living in Sheffield, but whenever she went to Yemen she was not expected to express her opinion in front of men. Her years at SOAS had given her a deeper understanding of her own culture, she felt.

I became curious about Sheffield and when I expressed my wish to see the town, Zeinab gave me her contact details and asked me to let her know when I planned to visit. She told me that the town had received much financial aid in the last few years to fund various projects so I would find plenty of interest there.

I hadn't been to Yorkshire before but I had heard about the kindness of its people. The county had also given its name to a pudding that I often heard mentioned by American visitors to London. I felt cheated when I finally tasted Yorkshire pudding for the first time. It was not a pudding at all but a kind of puffed pastry pie. My idea of a pudding was a sweet dessert dish. A bad-tempered American once asked me to recommend a restaurant. When I told him about the choice of restaurants in the neighbourhood, he was offended that I didn't mention any which served traditional English food. He asked me whether I would send someone visiting Kashmir to an American-style fast food restaurant. He was absolutely intent on eating Dover Sole and Yorkshire pudding that evening.

I phoned Zeinab a week before my intended visit. She gave me her address and said that I could meet her at her home. I decided to travel there a day before and stay overnight, having arranged to meet Zeinab around noon.

There was a limited service between London and Sheffield on a Sunday afternoon. Usually I bought my train ticket on the day of travelling but this time I had booked it in advance. It was the first time I'd taken a train out of St Pancras. Since there was only one Underground station for Kings Cross and St Pancras, I hadn't realized until many months after my arrival in London that these were two different stations above ground. I was surprised to see the train full on a Sunday afternoon. Then it occurred to me that many of the passengers were returning home after spending a weekend in London. The first-class coaches looked welcoming, with cups laid upside-down on the tables for tea and coffee. However, most of the passengers were heading towards the standard coaches.

I had expected delays due to the maintenance work carried out on Sundays. But the train departed on time. The announcer stated that there would be no trolleys going round with drinks and snacks due to equipment shortages. He offered passengers the option of getting a hot or cold drink from the snacks counter in one of the coaches. I wanted to grab a drink and passed through several coaches on my way to the coach between first and standard classes where the drinks were served. A long queue of people had already formed. The man serving the drinks was apologetic about the delay, telling everyone that they were "the best" and he was "the worst".

It was dark by the time the train reached Sheffield. The town centre was quiet on a Sunday evening. I decided to walk to the hotel since it was not too far from the station. But I didn't have a map of the town so I asked various people for directions on my way to the hotel. They were friendly enough but didn't seem to know exactly where the hotel was located. I walked for about half an hour until someone told me that I had already passed it. I turned back and walked for a mile until I found the hotel in a quiet residential area. Perhaps that was why people didn't know its location. My room for the night was bigger than I expected. When I entered, I found the windows slightly open and the air in the room was fresh.

It was easier for me, having been lost the night before, to find my way to the town centre in the morning. I walked downhill past a cemetery with a derelict church at its entrance. Sheffield's landscape isn't flat. The edges of the town are picturesque but the town centre has many tower blocks within it. The town is well signposted for cyclists but none were in sight that day.

Zeinab had asked me to meet her near the Millennium Galleries, opposite the Central Library. I passed a few nondescript buildings until I reached a fine building made of Derbyshire stone, with a terraced garden. The building looked incongruous in its drab setting. When I reached the entrance, I realized that it was the town hall. I saw a Union Jack flying on top of another landmark building to the right of the town hall and this turned out to be the Central Library. I had passed a glasshouse-type structure without knowing that it led to a galleria. The glasshouse, recently opened by the Queen, contained a winter garden with many species of tropical plants.

I waited for Zeinab near the entrance of the glasshouse. When I met her she told me she had been to the Central Library in the morning for a couple of hours and wanted me to see it before we went to the other side of the town. It looked very substantial compared to the structure built opposite to celebrate the new Millennium. It had more than one reading room on the ground floor and Zeinab showed me the main one, where she had been that morning, a spacious, neatly laid out facility. She told me that she came here once or twice a week to update herself on current affairs. I asked her if there was a coffee-shop in the library where we could have a chat. But she insisted that I visit her home as her mother had made some sweets for us to eat with our coffee.

We walked past the town hall towards Sheffield's cathedral. An unfamiliar experience for me, in England, was the sight of trams moving along one of the roads. Zeinab's flat was on the ground floor of a big block of flats. It was a two-bedroom flat that Zeinab's father had bought more than twenty years ago. In the living-room were an oriental-style divan and two armless chairs. There were bolsters and cushions on one side of the room for those who preferred to sit on the floor. In one corner was a large brass plate of an intricate design with bric-à-brac placed on top of it. I asked Zeinab about the function of an earthenware pot painted in bold colours. She said that it was used in Yemen to burn incense. A knife with a carved handle and a decorative sheath was displayed on one of the walls, as well as a few family pictures. One of them was a group photograph of the graduates of the Royal Military Academy at Sandhurst, taken in the 1950s. Zeinab told me that her father had graduated from Sandhurst but had never actually joined the army in Yemen. He came from a well-to-do family in Aden who thought of sending their son to Sandhurst to gain respectability among their people. There was also a photograph of a woman in her twenties whose head was covered by a white scarf. It was Zeinab's younger sister, who had married in Yemen ten years ago and was now living with her husband in Dubai.

Zeinab had been to Yemen to attend the wedding. She realized there that her relatives didn't like the idea of a younger sibling marrying first. They thought she was breaking a tradition and were expecting her to marry soon.

What was Zeinab's opinion of Yemeni people living in Sheffield? It was an invisible community, she said, and apart from producing a successful bantam-weight boxer the Yemenis in town remained unknown. Many of their men still went to Yemen to marry women who would dutifully follow them to Sheffield. Zeinab was too independent-minded for these men. She worked tirelessly to give voice to her community but expected very little in return. She said that some of the older Yemeni men would bring wives back from Yemen young enough to be their daughters.

What did Zeinab's mother have to say about her work? She would have preferred her to marry like her younger sister. She thought that education for woman in Yemen was more a hindrance than an advantage when it came to looking for a match. Many men in Yemen considered Zeinab over-qualified.

Although she disliked this label she thought that there was a measure of truth in it. On her last visit to Sana'a some of the men had asked her absurd questions. Zeinab's mother spent the winter months in Dubai with her younger daughter. But Zeinab herself couldn't spend more than a few days there. She found the idea of living in a city like Dubai very far from reality. She couldn't understand why so many wealthy Arab men came to Dubai and spent so much money there.

Zeinab's mother had gone to a nearby town in the morning to see one of her cousins. Sometimes, however, she stayed at home for weeks on end. It was Zeinab who did the shopping but her mother always cooked for both of them. It gave Zeinab more time for her voluntary job. She also brought work home much of the time and worked late at night.

I asked her what their family life was like when her father was alive. Her father had remained loyal to the King, Zeinab said, even after he was deposed. Many of his own people had betrayed him and benefited from the coup. There were people in Aden who hated British rule, fighting guerrilla-style warfare against the British soldiers. Her father hadn't taken part in this fight against imperial rule, even though he knew that some of those who were fighting for independence regarded him as a traitor. So when the King was overthrown her father had left the country and come to live in Sheffield. He had died at the age of fifty-two. When he was alive they would fly to Paris twice a year for shopping. Then, towards the end of his life, he started to run out of money. They would have fallen on hard times if her father hadn't bought a couple of properties in Sheffield. They had another flat, which they rented out and it helped them get by.

I was curious about what inspired Zeinab to do voluntary work. She said that her community's situation filled her with such despair that she felt impelled to do something for them. She could understand their helplessness through the life of her own mother. How far had she succeeded in accomplishing her task? Zeinab said that it was just the beginning and thought it might take her a lifetime to see a real improvement in their condition.

Zeinab wanted me to try the sweets made by her mother and invited me to have a coffee made from beans grown in Yemen, recently brought back by her cousin. While Zeinab was grinding the beans in her kitchen, the aroma of the ground coffee travelled to the living room and had a therapeutic effect on me. She served the coffee in very small cups with a gilt rim. The sweets made by her mother proved to be an excellent accompaniment.

Some time after leaving Zeinab's place, I decided to visit one of the Millennium Galleries, which had an exhibition of cutlery made in Sheffield. I passed a hotel known as *Cutlers* on my way and saw beyond the galleries a newly-built university made of concrete and glass. I wanted to grab something to eat before entering the metalwork gallery. There was a coffee-shop inside, full of office workers wearing pinstripe suits. My order was taken by a uniformed waitress whom I'd seen serving chips with a portion of sandwiches to someone sitting at the next table. I fancied trying this unusual combination myself. A blue napkin on the table, I noticed, had these words printed on it: 'There were some wonderful cutlery companies in Sheffield.'

In the sixteenth century three out of five Sheffield men were cutlers. The Company of Cutlers was formed in Hallamshire by an Act of Parliament. It had the power to issue cutlers' marks, enrol apprentices and impose fines on those who made cutlery of poor quality. In the eighteenth century Sheffield's metalwork industry began to expand and by the middle of the century Sheffield products had reached Russia and America. By the 1850s the knives and forks produced in Sheffield were being exported as far as New Zealand, South Africa, the West Indies and South America. Sheffield's control of the world market for cutlery was expressed in verse:

> 'Through all Europe we're known
> To the Indies our goods go
> Through Afric' they are shown.'

It was only at the beginning of the twentieth century that Sheffield's market was overtaken by Germany, which used more advanced manufacturing processes. By the 1930s America had become the world's largest manufacturer of cutlery, with Germany second and Sheffield third.

The gallery had an interesting display of cutlery in a multitude of shapes. Some of the old knives on display had broken ends. The explanatory text on the wall stated two possible reasons for this. One was that these were poor quality blades collected by the wardens of the Cutlers Company in London, who regulated the industry. They then defaced the blades so that they could not be sold again. The other explanation was that London cutlers broke Sheffield-made knives to protect their business from their rivals.

There was also a range of penknives on display in the gallery. The penknife was originally the name for a knife with a delicate blade used to cut and shape a quill into a pen. Penknives were first made in Sheffield in the eighteenth century and were eventually superceded when metal nibs were introduced.

A menacing display of hunting knives occupied one of the walls. These knives were exported from Sheffield in large numbers at the beginning of the nineteenth century and were very popular with American frontiersmen. The blades of these knives were etched with patriotic slogans like 'The United States / the Land of the Free and Home of the Brave / Protected by her Brave and Noble Volunteers.'

It was disconcerting to see in the gallery an array of fork handles made of ivory. In the nineteenth century vast quantities of elephant tusks were imported to satisfy the demand for ivory handles. One of the cutlery companies was using fifteen tons of ivory each year.

It was the metal industry that had shaped the landscape and fortune of Sheffield. In the 1860s Sheffield reached the peak of its trade with America and was expanding its market throughout the world. It manufactured 50% of the steel made in Europe. The decline of the town began after World War II. There were massive redundancies in the metal industry in the 1970s due to world competition.

The town had received much funding for regeneration projects. But it retained the grim look of '60s and '70s tower-block architecture. As for the Yemeni people living in Sheffield, they did not have the trading skills possessed by other migrants. Very few of them had succeeded in running their own businesses and their community had indeed become virtually invisible.

The next-door gallery displayed metal treasures that I had no inclination to see. Another gallery had a collection of works by John Ruskin, who had wanted to improve the working lives of people in Sheffield. I left the metalwork gallery after having learnt the etymology of the word 'hallmark' – a mark issued by Goldsmith's Hall in London.

I went back to the library across the road to see its art gallery on the top floor. One of the rooms had a statue carved in brilliant white marble, in the likeness of a Rodin masterpiece, by a contemporary sculptor. There was also a painting of an unemployed man in pensive mood. It was from the 1930s and a stark reminder of the times. A small painting by RB Kitaj titled *The Rival Poet* reminded me of an enigmatic tapestry work based on his painting *If Not, Not* in the British Library, in which a man wearing a jacket and tie is lying on the grass close to the contours of a female breast.

On leaving the library, I saw a sign mounted on a post with 'Cultural Industries Quarter' printed on it. The name struck me as bizarre and I later found it to be the location of the National Centre for Popular Music. I remembered Zeinab telling me earlier that a lot of money was being spent to regenerate the area around the train station. Perhaps this was one of those projects.

I drifted towards a pedestrianized street known as The Moor. Many of its shops looked like discount stores. There were also market stalls in the street. I was puzzled to see wheelchairs on sale at these stalls.

Zeinab had given me the name of someone who worked in one of the shops in The Moor. Omar was from Somalia and had come to live in Sheffield six years ago. He looked like a BBC journalist of the same name. He smiled when I mentioned it, saying that, unlike him, the BBC journalist was a very clever man. Omar had a wife and two children in Somalia whom he hadn't seen since he'd left for London. He had thought of bringing them over in the beginning but the prospects of it happening appeared slim to him now. He was very saddened by the civil war in Somalia. I asked him what had made him come to Sheffield rather than some other town. Omar said that one of his friends from

Somalia was living in Sheffield at the time, though he had since moved to Birmingham. There were not many Somalis living in Sheffield but Omar had found friends among the Yemenis. Zeinab's cousin was a close friend.

Omar was taller than his namesake at the BBC and showed brilliantly gleaming teeth when he laughed. I asked him if he had been to London in the last six years. Yes, he had been to Ealing in West London a few times. There were many Somalis living around Ealing. When he was there, he felt that Somalis were disliked by the Punjabis and Gujaratis who had settled in the area two decades before them. The Asian traders considered Somalis to be idle and were nervous when they saw a group of Somali men loitering outside a place of worship. Some of them had moved to other neighbourhoods after the arrival of Somalis in the area.

Omar wanted to work for himself but didn't have the capital to open a business. He thought, with grim irony, that the solution to world poverty was to increase the daily grind. When one travels from a poor country to a rich country, he said, one becomes a workhorse in order to guarantee the freedoms of affluent people. It demoralized him to see how Gujaratis were running their businesses in the UK. Many of these businessmen had become bitter as a result of working long hours and judged others by how many properties they owned. The Somalis could offer no competition to these seasoned traders other than running rundown Internet cafés in poor neighbourhoods of London. Most of the Somali men were employed in low-paid jobs while their women were raising children at home.

Omar had worked in the discount shop for three years, he said. He had wanted to pick up the skills to open his own shop but now he was having second thoughts. It was a risky business and hard to survive in it unless one had the support of family and friends. He was probably right. I had seen quite a few discount shops opening overnight in London and then disappearing after a few months. One of these businessmen told me that he always rented his shop on a very short-term lease and paid his rent weekly. He had moved his business five times in as many years. In one year he vacated his shop twice and then rented it back from the landlord who was asking for an increase in rent. He paid a very high rent because of the short-term lease. He had also declared himself bankrupt once business became very tough. A few months later he opened a new shop in someone else's name.

Omar had realized that it was difficult for him to open a shop on his own even though he had learned the tricks of the trade. He was now looking for a job in a supermarket to avail himself of the benefits of working for a big company. He would have to start at the bottom until he gained some experience and perhaps become a supervisor one day. One has to do all kinds of jobs, he said, to send a little money home. He could also save on the cost of food if he worked in a supermarket. There was very little benefit working for a small business, he thought, except when the owner occasionally felt generous and handed out a little money to his employees.

I asked Omar what he thought of the Somalis living in West London. He said that many of them worked very hard for their meagre wages. But they would become extravagant when they got married and hire an expensive venue for their wedding. I had been to one or two Somali weddings and seen bride and groom sitting on throne-like chairs. Omar said that if the money is earned by sweat, one shouldn't be lavish in spending it. Somalis living in West London shouldn't forget the poverty at home.

It was time for me to say goodbye and take a train back to London. I walked towards the big university building to reach the train station. There was so much roadwork going on around there that it was difficult to cross over to the other side of the street.

As the train pulled towards London and the sun set behind the dales I thought about the rise and fall of the metal industry in Sheffield and how the town had attracted a few thousand people from the Arabian Peninsula. The importance of Aden as a British Crown colony had diminished after the Suez Canal was nationalized by Nasser. The history of the British Empire was intertwined with commercial interests and the importance of a colonial town depended on how much revenue it generated for the mother country by way of trade and commerce. In Sheffield I had seen some of the remnants of that once all-pervading imperial enterprise.

Second City of the Empire – Glasgow

I caught a glimpse of Glasgow for the first time from a motorway while travelling by coach from Edinburgh to Stirling. The cityscape was dominated by brown and beige tower blocks. Having been to Edinburgh a few times, I was keen to visit its less buoyant neighbour. I remembered having met Jaspal in London a few years earlier, who told me that he worked for his uncle in Glasgow. I searched for his phone number, which I had written on a scrap of paper, but failed to find it. Then a few weeks later, looking for something else, I found it inside an envelope in my desk drawer. I wasn't sure if he still lived there but I was in luck. When I phoned Jaspal, he told me that although he was no longer working for his uncle he still lived in Glasgow and I should come and see him if I visited the town.

I travelled by Great North Eastern Railways to Glasgow via Edinburgh, the farthest I had ever travelled in the British Isles. It was a five and a half hour train journey from London to Glasgow. I had travelled by train from New York City to Cheektowaga in Upstate New York and it had admittedly taken eight hours. But having got used to living in a small country, I was accustomed to short distances between cities and so the train ride from London to Glasgow seemed unduly long. I noticed some of my fellow passengers engaged in solving a Japanese puzzle in a newspaper. They even sought each other's advice in finding a solution. The man sitting in the opposite seat told me that he was going to see his parents in Edinburgh. He had moved to Richmond in London a few years ago. When I told him I was going to Glasgow, he said he hadn't been there for more than ten years. He told me that Glasgow was laid out like a grid yet he tended to get lost there. He found it easier to orientate himself in Edinburgh with its Castle overlooking the town.

Leaving the Central Station in Glasgow from the western exit, I was surprised to see a big pawnbroker just outside the station and a betting shop a few yards down the road. I asked a newspaper vendor for directions to my hotel but failed to grasp what he said. I apologized for being unable to understand him. He said it again but I still couldn't pick it up. Too embarrassed to ask him a third time, I nodded my head in false affirmation before walking away from him. It is certainly a mistake to ask a newspaper vendor for directions when one is not familiar with the Glaswegian tongue. As it happens, I had trouble in London for many years in distinguishing Scottish persons from Irish.

I asked a taxi driver who had parked his cab further along that road for directions to my hotel. He told me that

I'd pass "a wee lane" before reaching the hotel. I wondered what kind of road a wee lane was. I passed a hotel across the road built in an outlandish modern design. A uniformed porter in the lobby of this hotel was polishing his trolley, constructed in the shape of a birdcage. I passed another pawnbroker along the way. Strangely, air rifles and swords were displayed on one side of the shop and musical equipment such as guitars and record players were on the other side.

The hotel was located just before the intersection of the motorway from which I had caught a glimpse of the town a few years ago. The name of this road, Argyle, was spelt with an 'e' at the end whereas it was spelt with a double 'll' as a street name in Central London. Someone told me the next day that it was a mistake on the part of the sign-writer a century ago and it had been misspelt ever since. What he said sounded plausible until I discovered that many streets in London were named Argyle.

The staff at the hotel were friendly. It had begun to rain and the helpful receptionist lent me an umbrella for the evening. I left the hotel to walk back to the station and then to the East End of the town where Jaspal and I had arranged to meet. The shops became imposing after I crossed Union Street. Since it was closing time, people were on their way home carrying bulging shopping bags. The street had begun to empty except for a gathering of tramps, some of whom carried a mixture of drinks in plastic bottles. A sole bookshop among the numerous shoe shops displayed a 'Lease for Sale' sign above its entrance. One of the nearby buildings was covered in a giant canvas advertising a miniature electronic gadget. Mounted on a lamppost was a sign in cut-out letters which read 'Merchant City'. I walked towards a narrow tower in the middle of a road intersection. The luminous blue of its clock was visible from a distance in the dark. The part of town beyond the tower was dimly lit.

Jaspal had asked me to meet him in a restaurant under an iron bridge near the clock tower. Wanting to take a stroll in the East End of the town before our encounter, I turned right into Saltmarket to discover tenements made of stone. The shops at the street level of these tenements were fitted with metal shutters, two or three shutters fitting side by side over their glass windows. In between the shops were entrances to the tenements. I returned to the clock tower and drifted into another road. An old man who seemed to have recently emerged from a desolate pub was lying outside on the pavement and two passers-by were trying to help him up. I remembered a London journalist I'd once met telling me that there was a place near Glasgow where the average life expectancy of men and women is drastically below the national average. When he visited the town he had found many of its residents drenched in alcohol. Perhaps it wasn't such a good idea to wander around the East End of Glasgow in the dark. I decided to wait for Jaspal in the restaurant.

I didn't have to wait long. After greeting each other

I asked him about his new job. He told me he'd been working in a clothes shop since leaving his uncle's business. He also worked at the Barras Market at the weekends. His uncle didn't pay him very much. Although he used to work over eighty hours a week, his uncle paid him under two hundred pounds. No matter how many hours a week he worked he received a fixed amount. Then he learned he was being paid just half of the minimum wage. He felt that he had wasted time working for his uncle.

When he was very young Jaspal had dreamt of leaving his village and returning one day as a wealthy man. He counted himself lucky to have an uncle in Glasgow. Jaspal came from a Sikh family in Punjab. However, unlike most Sikh men, he did not wear a turban, having cut his hair short when he moved to Glasgow. He intended to grow his hair again before returning to his village as he wouldn't feel comfortable there without wearing a turban. But he had felt out of place wearing a turban in Glasgow. Unsure how his elders would feel if they saw him with short hair, he hadn't sent a photo of himself to his parents for two years. He also told me that he had become a teetotaller. Sikhs were forbidden to smoke but many of their men were accustomed to alcohol. He wanted to stay away from the bottle in case he become like his uncle, whom he had seen drinking a bottle of whisky a day and ending up stupefied late at night. Jaspal considered himself fortunate not to have followed in his uncle's footsteps. Every morning when he went to work he would come across men in the street who started their day by drinking and loitering outside fast food restaurants. All of them were unfit to work and depended on the state to meet their needs. He took fright at this common sight in Glasgow and decided to stay away from pubs in the evening.

So what did he do for his social life in Glasgow? He didn't socialize much in the town, he said, except for meeting one or two students from Punjab who were attending a course there. Jaspal said that he wouldn't be able to fulfil his dream of building a house in his village if he socialized in Glasgow. So he mostly kept himself busy by working extra hours. Had he been to any other town in Scotland, like Edinburgh or Stirling? No, he'd never been anywhere else, as he was working seven days a week. How exhausting was that? He said that people who worked five days a week found it difficult to comprehend how someone could work throughout the week. But he hadn't found it too difficult to get into the routine of working without taking a day off.

Weekend trading in the Barras Market provided him with a break from his weekday job. It also gave him a chance to earn a bit more than the hourly rate. He didn't pay for the merchandise, which was provided by the owner of the shop he worked for during the week. The market stall helped the shopkeeper to get rid of his seconds. Although he earned only a bit more than his usual wage, it gave him a sense of freedom to run his own stall. He had also found other stallholders very friendly. Some of them called him Jasper and others found it easier to call him Paul. But he didn't mind them calling him by a different name. He had discovered camaraderie among the market traders. For instance, they kept an eye on his stall if he had to use the toilet. Jaspal felt good to be able to give money from the sale of merchandise to the shopkeeper, who was also his boss on weekdays.

Jaspal aimed to save forty thousand pounds to build a house in his village in Punjab. He reckoned it would take him two more years to achieve that goal. Working throughout the week had helped him to control his expenditure. He wanted to settle down after building a house in his village. His uncle had married a Glaswegian woman twenty years ago but they had no children and his uncle's wife was also dependent on alcohol. Jaspal considered it important for him to marry someone from his own caste.

Jaspal's life in Glasgow reminded me of the time during the first Gulf War, when Indian labourers were being evacuated from Kuwait, that I had flown via a Middle Eastern country to New Delhi. The plane was boarded by many labourers returning home with a little money and electronic gadgets. They had denied themselves every pleasure in order to return home with their savings. Several of them asked me to fill out their disembarkation cards for them. They had endless trouble in clearing their baggage through customs. One of them burst into tears when questioned by a customs officer. It was heart-rending to witness that scene.

It was half past eight when I said goodbye to Jaspal to

go back to my hotel. I passed the clock tower on the way to the Central Station. Outside the station one of the usual American fast food outlets was besieged by a group of youngsters. I was looking for somewhere to eat when I saw a sign outside a pub advertising curry. The place was crowded. I ordered food at the bar and waited for it sitting in a corner far away from the smokers. But soon the whole area was full of smoke. I would have left the place if I hadn't already ordered the food, which arrived a few minutes later. As it turned out, the lentils tasted better than what I was used to eating in Indian restaurants in London.

Wherever I had travelled in Britain, from the Peak District to the Lake District, an Indian restaurant could always be found. I once met a Bengali man in London who planned to open an Indian restaurant in a town in Britain which had none. It had proved to be quite a challenge to find such a town. Many of the names of Indian restaurants in Britain evoked sour memories of the empire. Some of them were named after jingoists like Kipling and others were named after Queen Victoria – the Empress of India. Even the uniforms of the waiters were reminiscent of the Raj. It seemed to me like an extension of the Raj that Bengali chefs were cooking food in Indian restaurants for their English patrons just as the Khansamas in India cooked English food for their masters.

I had seen only the East End of Glasgow the night

before and wanted to see other parts of the town. On the following morning I left the hotel and walked toward the River Clyde to see Glasgow Harbour and get to know better what was known as the Second City of the Empire. The quay on the south side of the Clyde was originally built in the seventeenth century when it traded in fish, coal, salt and hides with France and Ireland. Trade expanded after the Union of England and Scotland, which gave Scottish merchants free access to colonial markets. A great boom in tobacco and sugar followed, bringing wealth to Glasgow merchants who built large mansions to the west of the town. This trade collapsed after Britain lost America as a colony.

The River Clyde offered a bleak prospect, with huge rusting cranes dominating its quayside. One could see the shiny metal roof of a distant building designed in the shape of an armadillo. It looked as if the metal structures of the Thames Barrier at Woolwich had been joined together to resemble an insect-eating mammal. When I walked closer to this structure, I discovered that it was an auditorium. There was a Science Centre nearby, built in the middle of a car park bordered by a motorway. I passed a helipad, beyond which was anchored an old ship as a tourist attraction. The landscape was open and windswept and it felt as if I was strolling at the wrong end of the town. I walked hastily back towards Argyle Street.

I wanted to walk around George Square to see the architecture for which I had heard Glasgow is famous.

I turned into Union Street after passing the Central Station. The street was jammed with buses. I found it irksome to walk in a city laid out like a grid. There was a traffic light at every corner and one had to be very mindful of traffic before crossing the road.

When I reached George Square I saw a statue mounted on a tall column in the middle of the square. It represented Walter Scott. I was glad that Glasgow, unlike London, had chosen a writer rather than an admiral to preside over the populace in its main square. The architecture of the building around George Square looked very grand. The heads of horsemen cast in bronze were messy with pigeon droppings. Although it was only October, workmen were already putting up Christmas lights around the square.

Walking around the town, it occurred to me that Glasgow had hosted the Empire Exhibition in 1938, a year before the war that eventually put paid to the Empire. It had attracted a huge number of visitors. By the time the exhibition was mounted, Glasgow had already lost its status as a great city. I had seen pictures of the exhibition with a futuristic tower at its centre. But hardly anything of the exhibition had survived. And the workshops of Glasgow, building ships for the Empire, had gone into irrevocable decline.

A few of the signs above the shops around town were written in the style of Charles Rennie Mackintosh. The lettering of these signs was tall and thin and looked similar to the high-backed chairs he designed. Glasgow attracts students of architecture to see examples of Mackintosh's work, among others. An American woman who admired his work once told me that he was treated badly by his own government, who suspected him of espionage during the First World War.

In London, an elderly Scottish woman who delighted me with her stories always mentioned Glasgow University when she talked about the town. Built on a hill overlooking the town is one of the oldest universities in the country, founded in 1492 when Columbus set out on his journey to the East Indies and discovered the New World. At the time of my visit, the autumn landscape was very vivid, as if an artist had painted a canvas in warm colours. I walked along Sauchiehall Street, whose Scottish name someone translated for me as 'meadow of the willow trees'. Glasgow University reminded me of Adam Smith and his book, *The Wealth of Nations*. He had taught Logic and Moral Philosophy at this university.

A building with domed roofs turned out to be the hospital known as The Royal Infirmary. It was interesting that hospitals were once called infirmaries. This word came to my mind again when I saw the men and women around the Central Station wrecked by drink, unable to walk upright. They were truly infirm. Also giving pause for thought was a cemetery at the other end of the town known as Necropolis.

I wanted to take a bus to Paisley after roaming the streets of Glasgow but the hotel concierge told me it was easier to take a train there. I had heard this place-name often from the shawl sellers in Kashmir. They attributed the name to a Kashmiri motif embroidered on the woollen shawls. But the craftsmen and weavers in Kashmir who produced shawls knew this motif by a local name. For some time, I considered this swirling teardrop (or palmette) design to be a British import. Then I learnt that the weavers in Paisley had in fact copied this design from the shawls produced in Kashmir. So when I came to London, I very much wanted to visit the town that had given its name to a Kashmiri design motif.

The train left the Central Station and stopped at a few places before reaching Paisley. One could find ethnically diverse faces here and there in Glasgow but Paisley was completely homogenous, judging from the people who alighted there. I suddenly became self-conscious walking along the platform. A group of youngsters booed me from the other platform. However, when I asked a shop assistant for directions to the museum, she was kind enough to escort me out of the station and point me in the right direction.

The museum was only a short distance from the station. It was sunny and the mellow stone museum building was basking in the afternoon sun. The first flight of steps led to a reception area and the second to its main gallery. There were banners hanging from the banisters promoting children's activities in the museum. A few women were traversing the main gallery with small children. When I entered the main gallery, I found a display of working-class life in Victorian Paisley. An explanatory text stated that the middle classes often viewed the working classes as poor managers of their domestic affairs. A century ago many books were published on household management and cookery for the poor. These ideas were based on misunderstanding. For example, the well-off failed to see that it was not possible for the poor to buy food economically in bulk, because they had neither the income nor the storage facilities. It brought to mind the argument of people living in rich countries who say that the main cause of poverty in many poor countries is mismanagement by their governments.

In the gallery I saw one of the bicycles made by Kirkpatrick Macmillan, who built the first bicycle in 1839. It had a huge front wheel, with a saddle made of leather on top and a very small rear wheel. This came to be known as a 'penny farthing'. The bicycle was in good condition but one had to be as expert as a tightrope walker to ride it. Kirkpatrick Macmillan was a blacksmith by trade and applied the principle of hobby horses to bicycles with pedals. I felt most grateful to this Scotsman for his invention, which remains my preferred mode of transport.

The museum had a collection of other items made by Paisley firms, including a range of sewing threads manufactured by Coates and Anchor. This display reminded me of my uncle's shop in the old part of Srinagar, which was full of boxes containing sewing threads. His customers were mostly tailors from the city and shopkeepers from neighbouring villages.

The gallery had a display of photographs of a Paisley engineer, A F Craig, taken on his world tour in 1908. The museum described one of the photos of this big Scotsman, sitting on a rickshaw pulled by a lean oriental man in a uniform, as 'charming'. Until recently foreign travel for Paisley people was a luxury that only the rich could afford. For many people, foreign travel was likely to mean emigration, a separation from friends and family undertaken reluctantly in the hope of a better life, either in America or one of the colonies of the British Empire. The ordinary people of Paisley first experienced the wider world as a result of war, serving as volunteers, conscripts and regular servicemen.

When I walked around the gallery, I found a display, curiously labelled 'Curator's Office', which included a fine example of the taxidermist's craft in the form of colourful life-like birds perched on twigs. I was about to leave the museum when I asked the receptionist if it exhibited any shawls. I was glad that I enquired, because he told me there was a gallery behind the main gallery which had nothing but shawls displayed in it.

There was no one in the shawl gallery except an attendant sitting by a desk at the far end of the room. The shawls were hanging on one side of the gallery and there were mannequins clad in costumes that demonstrated changes of attire of women in Britain during the last three hundred years. In fact, it was changes of fashion that explained the rise and fall of the shawl industry in Paisley and Srinagar.

Artefacts at the gallery entrance explored the origins of the Paisley palmette motif. The display suggested this motif had originated in Mesopotamia and then travelled to Kashmir before the shawl weavers in Paisley adopted it as their characteristic pattern. I was surprised to learn that this motif had in fact come from the leaves of 'The Tree of Life'. Ancient trade routes linked Mesopotamia with the rest of Asia and Europe. It was along these routes that the palmette design from the sacred tree travelled and came to appear in the arts of many different cultures. In Europe, the palmette can be found in the distinctive swirls of Celtic art, although it was replaced by the representative arts of Greece and Rome. However, it was in Kashmir that the symbol was first used on a shawl-like garment. The weavers in Kashmir looked to nature for inspiration. They created textiles with the sacred leaf design for the Mogul rulers of India, who spent summer months in the cooler parts of the empire.

I'd believed that Kashmiri shawls became popular in France before reaching Britain. But the Paisley Museum suggested otherwise. It refuted the claim that the European fashion for shawls had begun after Napoleon's campaigns in Egypt in the 1790s, claiming that Kashmiri shawls acquired by East India Company men were already popular in Britain in the 1760s.

I saw an elegant dressing-gown in the gallery that had been created from a family-owned shawl of the 1860s. A Glasgow tailor had charged about forty pounds in 1975 to do the work and he actually commented at the time that it was "a piece fit for a costume museum". The tailor was indeed right. Its owner had worn it many times before the gown became a museum piece.

The gallery depicted the life of shawl weavers in Paisley using photographs and written text. Paisley had been a single-industry town and suffered at times as a result of changes in ladies' attire. Similarly, many shawl businessmen had risen and fallen in Kashmir with fluctuating demand for their wares. The Great War brought an increasing number of foreign visitors to Kashmir and created a few wealthy shawl-wallahs. Their fortunes had become legendary and I heard about it as part of the local folklore while growing up in Srinagar.

The museum was to close in fifteen minutes. Time had passed for me very quickly inside the shawl gallery. Before leaving, I asked the attendant about an empty space on the wall. She said that a Kashmiri shawl had been removed while repairs were made to the wall. She added that the museum had a collection of over a thousand shawls, only a handful of which were on display because of the limited space.

On my way out I saw a working loom in one of the rooms. The notice posted at its entrance stated that the weaver was on holiday. The room was full of different-coloured wool on spindles, with punched cards hanging over the raw material. It would have been interesting to see the weaver at work and transforming the holes in the cards into the intricate design on a shawl.

I left the museum and walked along Paisley High Street to get back to the train station. I thought of stopping somewhere for a coffee but then decided to catch the next train to Glasgow.

The Central Station was busy with evening commuters. I sat down in a coffee-shop inside the station to invigorate myself with a hot drink. I thought of seeing Jaspal again but didn't feel inclined to go to the East End of Glasgow again. So instead I spent the evening roaming around the town centre. I found a few Australians and New Zealanders working in various businesses around there. The woman who served me coffee was from the American south. Wanting to buy a newspaper before going back to my hotel, I entered a corner shop run by an Asian family. The man behind the counter seemed nervous while serving his customers. It reminded me of my own nervousness when working for an Asian newsagent in London. I had felt insecure knowing that I could lose my job any time and would be at a total loss in London without work.

Next morning I left the hotel to go to Edinburgh for the day. The man behind the ticket counter at the Central Station told me that I should go to Queen Street Station to catch a train. I had a vague idea where the station was located, having passed Queen Street the day before. I wondered if the street was named after a queen of Scotland or of England. I walked past Buchanan Street, famous for its shops. Glasgow claimed to be a shopper's paradise, second only to London. When I turned into Queen Street, I was surprised to find an army recruitment centre operating from a shop. Further up the road a neo-classical building housed the Gallery of Modern Art, and to prove it the pediment was adorned with a glaring example of its contents.

Trains to Edinburgh from Queen Street station were running frequently. I suddenly remembered what Glaswegians thought of Edinburgh. I had heard one of them say that the only good thing about Edinburgh is the train back to Glasgow.

Edinburgh Hospitality

When I finally found time and strength of will to go to Edinburgh, I had already spent seven years in London. I accompanied a friend there who was visiting the UK for a few days. He had hired a car on his arrival in London and wanted to drive up to Scotland. I was not keen on undertaking a long journey by car but I agreed to accompany my guest for the sake of courtesy.

We spent a good few hours on the motorway before passing Newcastle on the way and stopped for a late lunch at a petrol station. I was unfamiliar with these motorway facilities but my friend seemed at home there, having driven far and wide in his car.

We drove past small towns with charming names like Melrose and Jedburgh. The landscape became scenic when we reached the point that marks the old border between England and Scotland. However, this undulating landscape seemed denuded. It was not hard to guess that these hills must once have been covered with forests before they were cleared for agriculture. The sight of sheep grazing in the fields welcomes one to the countryside as soon as one travels out of London. But the narrow hilly road to Edinburgh brought me closer than usual to these submissive animals and their young. They reminded me of karakul caps made in Central Asia from the skins of newborn lambs. These caps are worn by older men in Kashmir as a mark of respect. As a child I was upset for many days when someone told me that the finest karakul pelts were often obtained from unborn lambs.

We passed the River Tweed, which has given its name to a woollen cloth synonymous in Britain with being an old-fashioned type but used widely in Kashmir to make winter clothing. Stone cottages built along the roadside advertised accommodation for tourists.

Edinburgh's landscape was less dramatic than I had imagined. The Pentlands did not offer me the spectacle of a mountainous landscape like the one I had conjured up, but I was captivated to see the city for the first time. I was familiar with a few Edinburgh street names, having heard them from the elderly Scottish lady I knew in London. The air of the town was crisp. It was early spring and I saw a few cyclists near Princes Street in summer gear. Then I came across a large group of them cycling in unison and realized that they were out for pleasure rather than commuting to work.

I had spent a good part of the day sitting in a car and yearned for a bike ride to stretch my legs. Our hotel was located out of town and it took us another half an hour to find it. After resting there for a while, we decided to go back into town. Most of the houses on the way were made of stone, as distinct from the brick houses of London. Having taken a wrong turn at a big roundabout we got lost for a while but finally found our way. My friend parked his car near the town centre and we decided to walk around to find a place to eat. There was a Chinese restaurant not far down the road, its interior painted in sea green. The restaurant was run by a young Chinese couple. The woman who welcomed us inside was very courteous and spoke with a Scottish accent. It was delightful to hear the soft Edinburgh tones issuing from the lips of a Chinese person.

I came back to the town in the morning. The first thing I wanted to do was climb Arthur's Seat, as I was eager to see the town from its summit. Since I lived in London, I hadn't climbed a mountain for many years but this was an easy ascent. I had often scaled higher peaks in Srinagar. Climbing up Arthur's Seat brought back memories of Solomon's Seat in Srinagar and a river below, flowing through the town. When I reached the summit of Arthur's Seat, it revealed the inlet of the North Sea with Fife on its far side. I would have liked to spend more time on the summit, just as I was accustomed to on Solomon's Seat, where I'd find a lake shimmering at its feet and sometimes catch the sun setting behind the high peaks to create an afterglow on the surface of the water. But it was very windy on Arthur's Seat so I decided to climb down. On my way back I came across a big group of joggers traversing the base of the small mountain. I didn't get a chance to explore the town on foot because my friend always drove around in his car.

I returned to Edinburgh that year during the summer. The town was full of tourists and one could see many youthful backpackers outside the main train station. The gardens along Princes Street were in full bloom. The town seemed very cheerful, probably because it was getting ready to host its annual festival in a few weeks time. The landscape reminded me of a ballad by Walter Scott that we were taught at school in Srinagar. I always faltered at the pronunciation of 'Lochinvar', the Scottish knight in the ballad. A few yards from the station I saw the sedentary figure of Walter Scott under a Gothic spire. Was the spire built to protect the writer from the elements, I wondered, or was it an abbey in which he had sought shelter? Further down the road I saw the statue of David Livingstone with a bible in one hand and a walking stick in the other.

Huge hotels, built in a lavish architectural style at both ends of Princes Street, suggested the popularity of Edinburgh as a tourist destination. Perhaps they provided accommodation for affluent Americans who came to the town to play a round of golf. At the hotel in London where I worked I had been asked by a few Californian guests to find a prestigious golf course for them in Scotland where their friends hadn't played. So I was familiar with the names of golf courses in Scotland even before I went there. I had also been asked about Muirfield (near Edinburgh) by a group of American businessmen who wanted to play a round there. When I dug out information for them, I was surprised to learn that women were not allowed in unless accompanied by men. I always marvelled at the golfers, who travelled thousands of miles with their outsize bags. It was a game which divided men into master and caddies. The men who carried the kit of their masters in India during the Raj were known as golf-coolies.

I was surprised to find how many hotels in London wanted to attract golfers. Perhaps it was because golfers tended to be well-heeled businessmen. Although those interested in golf constituted only a minority of its guests, London hotels took care to provide all the information they needed about golfing facilities in the town.

The hotel I stayed at in Edinburgh was surrounded by a golf-course. But I had no desire to play golf in Scotland, the birthplace of the game. I confused 'Tee Time', mentioned in the hotel brochure, with the time for tea. Golf is one of the most pretentious games played in the countries that were formerly British colonies. Membership of a golf-course in the Indian subcontinent is considered to be a social rank. I knew just one person in Srinagar who played golf. Whenever someone asked his family about his whereabouts, they were clearly fond of saying that he was at the golf course.

I used to see a man wearing a fez and a long black coat outside the golf-course in Srinagar soliciting European visitors for funds. He carried a cashbook in his attempt to convince them of his good deeds. One day he was noticed by a high official who was leaving the golf-course and ordered his arrest. A few days later, I saw the man in the fez again at a different location raising money for his causes.

It is the elitist character of golf which has perhaps made 'club' a loathsome word in India. One day I drifted on my bicycle into the Highgate Golf Course in North London to pick up some brochures for our hotel guests. The golfers raised their eyebrows when they saw me cycling towards the office. The course offered me a good vantage point for an interesting view of the neighbourhood. But I felt a strong need to get out of the vicinity of the golfers as soon as I'd picked up the leaflets.

The sight of heather and thistle growing in the wild around Edinburgh captivated me. I took a bus tour to Trossachs and Loch Lomond. When the bus passed Trossachs, I was reminded of a Wordsworth poem in which he describes the lake as more clear than glass. Indeed, it looked pristine. The sky was overcast when the bus reached Loch Lomond. I took a ride on the Loch with others in the group on a boat that looked like a fishing trawler. It felt so cold, even in July, that I zipped up my summer jacket. The Loch didn't look the way it was depicted on the posters of the

Scottish Tourist Board in the London Underground. These posters showed a smiling couple cycling along a road overlooking the Loch in perfect weather.

I wanted to see the Old and New town in Edinburgh during this, my second visit. When I reached Princes Street again in the morning, I found many visitors already perched on the ramparts of Edinburgh Castle. I decided to avoid the crowd at the castle and walk along the Royal Mile instead as I wanted to see views of the city through a camera obscura fitted at the top of a tower in the Mile. I was curious to see this simple optical device that had been used by Vermeer to create his masterpieces. There are also references to a Magic Lantern developed from a camera obscura in Proust's *À la recherche du temps perdu*. How interesting it was to see the play of light and shadows on a concave table creating the city scenes. But it was the attendant who truly brought these images to life with her playful commentary. She literally lifted some of these projected images with her dextrous hands to distort the scenes just as Proust distorted reality through his memory in his monumental work.

I left the tower to stroll along the Royal Mile. It was bizarre to see inside a church a display of photographs that tried to create an impression of apparitions – someone in London had once told me about the superstitious nature of Scottish people. A stone building with a random rubble-style exterior turned out to be a hotel. It had such small windows that I was curious to see what the rooms were like. The receptionist kindly offered to show me a room. Although the bedroom had old-fashioned furnishings, it looked new and I realized that the hotel had been recently built.

A few yards down the road I saw a group of American tourists leaning out of the top deck of a sightseeing bus. Then I saw their guide pointing towards a coffee-shop in which, he said, a certain contemporary author of children's books had started writing her first novel. Did the books of this children's writer appeal so much to these adults that they risked their lives by leaning out dangerously in a moving bus? Describing the Old Town, another tour guide was explaining the origins of the word 'loo' to an American group. According to him, when the medieval residents of the Old Town emptied their chamber pots into the street from the upper floors of tenements, they shouted "Regardez l'eau!". It seemed plausible to me. But when I later checked my Concise Dictionary it declared the origins of this word as uncertain.

A fifteenth-century house protruding into the Royal Mile had been turned into a museum for the mementos of the Presbyterian preacher, John Knox. When St. Andrew's Castle surrendered to the French in 1547, Knox was made a galley slave in France and later imprisoned. Of his time in exile Knox wrote: 'When the body was far absent from Scotland, my assured hope was, in open audience, to preach in St Andrews before I departed this life.'

The palace at the lower end of the Royal Mile was

besieged by tourists. I saw the new building of the Scottish parliament, designed by a Spanish architect. It didn't look as bizarre in its setting as it did in newspaper pictures. There are examples of neo-classical architecture everywhere in Edinburgh. When I saw the National Gallery of Scotland for the first time, it reminded me of an Athenian temple, except that it was built on low ground instead of a hill. I found later that its location was in fact known as The Mound.

I left the Old Town to walk along Edinburgh's shore. There were one or two couples pushing strollers along the road. I found it very mild, considering the latitude of the city. The Scottish lady in London had warned me that winters were colder in Edinburgh, which is why she preferred to spend the winter months in London. It was from her graciously refined manner that I had drawn an idea of the hospitality of Edinburgh people. I always found her soft tone and her turn of phrase delightful. One day she told me how the phrase 'daylight robbery' had come into use because of a tax on windows. I'd assumed it meant robbing people *in* the daylight rather than robbing them *of* the daylight.

The buildings of Edinburgh New Town reminded me of one of its architects, Robert Adams, who had remodelled a country house I often visited in London. It also reminded me of one of its earlier residents, Robert Louis Stevenson, who was dismissed by many critics for his 'simple' style of writing but was admired by great writers like Borges.

On my third visit to Edinburgh, I took a train from Queen Street station in Glasgow. It made a few stops on the way before reaching Waverly Station in Edinburgh. I saw London cabs driving in and out of the station and remembered the exit I had taken to reach Princes Street a few years earlier. The Old Town, which I had found breathtaking on my first visit, seemed familiar this time. Since it was mid-autumn, I didn't find as many tourists outside the station but there were several American tourists still about. I saw one family near the station getting to know another family. This was perhaps an American custom – introducing themselves to fellow-Americans when travelling in another country. A member of the family said that they were visiting their relatives in Scotland. Then they headed for a sightseeing bus.

I was going to meet an acquaintance in a coffee-shop in the Royal Mile. Peter, whom I'd met in London a few months earlier, was now employed in a hotel in Princes Street. A white South African, he had worked in the hotel for six months before deciding to move to Edinburgh. He had shared a one-bedroom flat in London with three other South Africans, who worked long hours during the day and then partied till late in the evening. They kept him awake by playing loud music in the flat. Peter wanted to rest in the evenings but the noise usually kept him awake. He would usually go to a supermarket every other day to buy food. But his flatmates consumed whatever he stored in the fridge. He also bought toiletries which everyone used without making a contribution. He was so fed up that he decided to move to Edinburgh to get away from his friends.

Peter wanted to save some money while working in the UK and then go back to South Africa. He missed his home terribly. But his friends were happy to spend whatever they earned in London on drinks and entertainment. Peter wanted to become a fireman on his return to South Africa and he also wanted to buy a pick-up van in Cape Town. He missed nothing more than the barbecues at his family home.

I had arranged to meet Peter in an American coffee-shop in the Royal Mile. I walked up a cobbled street, passing alleyways of the Old Town on my way. It was hard to imagine that at one time there were open sewers running through what was now a picturesque part of town. Peter met me outside the coffee-shop.

I asked him about his impressions of Edinburgh. He told me that he definitely preferred to live here rather than London. It had given him an opportunity to get away from his spendthrift friends. Besides, he had found London too full of distractions for him to save any money before going back to Cape Town. His friends often spent a week's wages in a few hours on a Friday night.

I had seen Edinburgh referred to in a travel guide as a great drinking city and was surprised that such an accolade could be conferred on a Presbyterian city. Peter said that drinking was the last thing that had attracted him to Edinburgh. He had left London in order to get away from the friends who constantly cadged money from him to spend in pubs. In fact, he found people in Edinburgh more sociable than Londoners. At least they reciprocated his own sociability.

Peter liked the fact that Edinburgh was much smaller than London. He didn't like spending two hours every day in London commuting between home and work. It took him only ten minutes by bus from the hotel where he worked in Edinburgh to his home. Sometimes he would walk instead and it took him only about half an hour. He found it hard to believe that people travelled to Central London from outer neighbourhoods at weekends and then spent a quarter of their weekly wages on a cab-ride home.

I had found South Africans living in London friendlier than most native Londoners. They didn't mind having a conversation with strangers. English people find it very odd, given their own comparative lack of sociability. An Englishwoman told me that she found South Africans in London very chatty. Although many of them had left their farm-houses to lead a one-room existence in London they didn't look miserable. They told me that the prospects of finding a job in South Africa were not good. And their currency was losing its value very fast.

Peter's friends in London considered him a workaholic, whose life-style filled them with dread. Besides, he was younger than many of them. He hadn't really grasped the changes which his country had gone through in the last fifteen years. He was only five years old when apartheid ended. White South Africans were travelling in large numbers to Britain and other countries in order to find work. Like other communities in London, the South Africans set up their own newspaper in the early 1990s. It mostly advertised temporary job vacancies. I had met many white South Africans in London but none from the black majority in the country – further proof, no doubt, of their deprivations during apartheid.

Peter found it upsetting that everything in South Africa was connected with politics. But that didn't diminish his love for the country. He was suffering the pangs of exile while living in the UK. I asked him if he'd managed to put some money aside while working in Edinburgh. He said he was certainly better off living on his own in Edinburgh than with his friends in London, who counted on him when they ran out of money in the middle of the week. He had been able to save more money in a few weeks than he had after six months in London. Was it actually cheaper for him to live in Edinburgh than London? He paid the same price for a cup of coffee in the Royal Mile as he paid in Central London. He also found the price of food very similar in the two cities. The rent he paid for accommodation was not that much cheaper than in London except that he shared his flat in Edinburgh with just two other people instead of four. He commuted to work by bus in Edinburgh as he did in London, so he couldn't reduce his travelling expenses. All in all, the only reason he was able to save money in Edinburgh was because his friends were not around.

What kind of work was he doing in the hotel in Edinburgh? He worked as a Room Service attendant, something he had done for a few weeks in London before moving to another department there. He didn't like working in Room Service in the London hotel, where he served meals mostly to English businessmen, some of whom considered him to be a bloody-minded foreigner. Peter told me that there is usually only one person working in Room Service in a big hotel in London, which is why the phone remains unanswered when that person is out delivering food to a room. However, the businessmen whom he usually served in London thought that Room Service was poor because the hotel employed foreigners, who are by definition inefficient. But they seldom appreciated it if the service was prompt. Peter said that tips are usually given *To Insure Prompt Service*. He had found Scottish people generous in comparison with the English. Those who order food to their rooms in London hotels, Peter said, should know that hospitality workers are mostly foreign because their own people consider working in a hotel as servile. One of the guests in London had complained to his manager that he had trouble in understanding him because of his Afrikaans accent. It had made Peter very sympathetic to the other members of the staff who came from Far Eastern countries and lacked confidence in the use of English. He found it upsetting that hotel Room Service had become subject matter for comedians in London. And he didn't mind if Scottish people didn't give him a tip when he took food to their rooms in Edinburgh because they were usually warm and friendly.

Peter's account brought to mind the hospitality of the Edinburgh lady in London who was in her mid-eighties but would insist on making a coffee for me whenever I visited her home. One day I told her that I was toying with the idea of moving to Edinburgh. She warned me about the city being less ethnically diverse than London. Perhaps it had worked better for Peter because he had been in London for only a few months and planned to return to South Africa after living in Edinburgh for a year.

Sometimes I would browse through the newspaper produced for London-based South Africans while I was waiting for a take-away in a restaurant that served barbecued chicken. I'd been introduced to one of these restaurants during my first year in London by a friend who told me that it was probably the best place to find an appetising grilled chicken. The newspaper usually weighed pros and cons in its features for South Africans wishing to return home. Peter had told me that he couldn't afford the price of a flight home during the holiday period, since so many South Africans were travelling.

Peter had left his girlfriend in South Africa when he came to London. He wanted to get back with her on his return to Cape Town. He said that South African women were very faithful when they were at home but he had seen them turning into social butterflies in London. Perhaps that was because they were less colour-conscious in London than they were in South Africa. Peter was glad that he hadn't socialized much in London; otherwise he would have ended up in debt like his friends, who needed a bank loan to buy a new pair of shoes.

Peter had become friendly with a chef from Holland in his hotel in Edinburgh. He understood a bit of Dutch because his ancestors came from Holland. The chef would make something in the hotel kitchen for him to eat if he felt hungry after finishing work. Peter had never actually been to Holland. It was easier for him to work in England because he felt more at home with English than with Dutch.

I asked him if he was still in touch with his friends in London. It seems that they spoke to him occasionally. They wanted to come to see him in Edinburgh but he couldn't ask them to stay at his place because his flatmate would mind. He had offered them rooms at a discount in the hotel where he worked. But they were not inclined to pay for accommodation when visiting their friend so they decided not to come. Peter was quite happy about that, knowing how much it would have cost to take care of them. Nor did he want to visit them in London in case they were hard up and asked him for money. Peter told me that they shouldn't be partying so often and then run out of money halfway through the week. His friends drowned their sorrows at leaving sunny South Africa by drinking late into the night. That was how they become oblivious of their pain.

London – An Imperial City

Some of the tailors who made suits for tourists in Srinagar claimed on their signboards to have been trained in London. It was my first impression of London: a capital city where the master tailors of the Empire were trained. I heard of Saville Row from a tailor in Kashmir who had given his business an amusing English name. But I failed to seek out this world-famous London street for many years. Then one day an American Senator staying in the hotel where I worked asked me to return a tailcoat and a top hat he had hired from a tailor in Saville Row. He seemed very sober in the mornings and had swollen eyelids, which always made me wonder how much he had drunk the night before.

I decided to go to Saville Row myself to return the outfit. I turned from Regent Street into Conduit Street and then found Saville Row on my left-hand side. A large building at the beginning of the street housed the offices of English Heritage. There were a few newly-built tailoring shops on one side of the road but the shop I was looking for was further down on the other side. When I entered the shop

I felt as if I'd travelled back in time, so strongly did the shop's interior create an illusion of the past. An elderly lady was working on an old manual typewriter. She got up as soon as she saw me enter. She knew that the costume I was returning had been hired by the Senator and asked me if he had been to the races at Ascot. In my turn, I asked her hesitantly to tell me more about the shop.

She told me it was one of the first tailoring shops to open in Saville Row and had been founded two centuries ago. Naturally, I was curious about who had been their clients during the last two hundred years. Their customers, she said, ranged from Anthony Trollope to Charles de Gaulle. What about the current state of the business? She sighed before saying that Saville Row was past its heyday. It wasn't like the old days. Some of the tailors in Saville Row no longer had workshops above or below their shops. So what had happened to their business? It was taken by the designer shops around the corner that were mostly selling foreign brands – Italian, French and even American. They had established their businesses recently and set out new trends in fashion. She said that many men nowadays were also getting their suits made in Hong Kong and Singapore.

I left the shop in Saville Row to have a look at other tailoring shops in the street. They were occupied by tailors who made suits mostly for men and therefore did not cater for one half of the population. It reminded me of a tailor in Srinagar who would tell his European and American clients that God had made him a man and he was going to make them a gentleman. Then he would hand them samples of corduroy and other fabrics and promise that they could go to a party "in a Park Lane hotel" wearing the suit he was going to make for them. I don't know if he had ever been to Park Lane or just heard about it.

I walked to the end of the road and then turned left. When I saw the Royal Academy, I realized how close Saville Row was to Piccadilly, which I walked up and down often though I had never drifted into the inner streets of Mayfair. When I passed Cork Street I remembered once meeting a struggling artist in Central London who told me she was going there to show her work to a gallery owner. A shopping centre beside the Royal Academy was used as a short cut by pedestrians. I reached Old Bond Street and found it livelier than Saville Row. It was here that I caught sight of a man dressed up like a nineteenth century dandy. He was strolling in a leisurely fashion and wielded a walking stick. At first I thought he was an elderly idler roaming the streets of Mayfair. He seemed to be a familiar figure as a few passers-by nodded to him. When I got closer, however, I was surprised to see that he was Asian. He reminded me of those East India Company men who wore tight formal clothing in the hot climes of Bengal and Madras. It seemed absurd for an Asian man to recreate such a decadent style in modern-day London.

Having reached Piccadilly, I turned towards Hyde Park for a stroll. I remembered seeing for sale a big display of reproduced paintings of English landscapes and horses on the pavement along this road during my first few months in London. The paintings had gilt frames as garish as the reproductions. It was near Hyde Park Corner that London seemed most like an imperial city to me. The triumphal arch with a chariot above and artillery around was surely a celebration of imperialism. The memorial gates at the beginning of Constitution Hill, which leads to Buckingham Palace, have the names of erstwhile colonial countries engraved on their pillars, like the various destinations which appear at the entrance of Euston Station.

I had seen many names in London similar to those of New Delhi, the architectural creation of Edwin Lutyens. For instance, I was surprised to find a hotel in Bloomsbury called The Imperial, which reminded me of its namesake in New Delhi. The Imperial Hotel in London was ugly but the one in Delhi was quite pleasing to the eye. Likewise, the Odeon cinema in Marble Arch brought to mind a cinema of the same name in New Delhi – was Oscar Deutsch responsible for entertaining our nation as well during the Raj? I had always felt ill at ease on finding various businesses in India using the word 'Imperial' in their company name. I hoped that the perpetrators were unaware of its connotations rather than deliberately evoking nostalgia for the Raj.

Some big companies in India were using abbreviations like ITC and ICI instead of 'Imperial Tobacco Company' or 'Imperial Chemical Industries' in order to hide their origins.

But I expected this adjective to have gone out of fashion in London. However, I found many businesses and institutions still using it. I wasn't sure what to make of 'Imperial College' until someone told me that it was one of the leading institutions for scientific research in the country. On the other hand, though I disliked the idea of a war museum, I didn't mind London's being called the 'Imperial War Museum'.

I decided that it was time to pay a visit to Greenwich again. I had been to Greenwich during my first summer in London eleven years earlier. It was a sunny day and turned out to be like a picnic for me. When I climbed up a hill to reach the observatory, I found it crowded with people taking pictures, with their feet apart, in front of a building. I wondered why they were so keen on taking pictures standing on an imaginary line. The next day I mentioned my 'picnic' in Greenwich (pronouncing it 'Green-itch') to a neighbour who corrected me by saying that the place is called 'Grenitch'.

It was the beginning of my humiliating journey through the realm of an unfamiliar language. Misunderstanding the ambiguous, sometimes fork-tongued character of the English language led me into abject situations while living in London during the next ten years. I was quite moved at first when someone told me as she took her leave, "See you around". I had taken the meaning of these farewell words literally. Then I realized some time later that 'around' was a vague abstraction and in fact I might never see that woman again. Sometimes I heard a native speaker mimicking my flawed pronunciation, trying to make others laugh in front of me without realizing how insensitive it was.

I took solace in reading. No, not English literature but works of French and Spanish authors whom I admired, translated into English. And then I played with the idea of writing, only to find out that my English wasn't up to scratch. I wasn't sure what was more bewildering, to pick up a new language or acquaint oneself with a new culture, until someone told me it amounted to the same thing.

On this, my second visit to Greenwich, I decided to go by boat, instead of taking a train, so I went to the pier near the Tower of London. I had been to Tower Hill many times but never thought of visiting the Tower of London. It was teeming with people even in December. I locked my bicycle in a rack and headed towards the pier. An immaculately dressed Beefeater was walking towards the Tower and was merrily greeted by many of the tourists.

The boat to Greenwich was bigger than those cruising between the Tower of London and Westminster. It was more like a commuter vessel than a sightseeing boat. There was even a counter for refreshments. It was also fitted with long electrical heaters. But there were only a few people taking the trip. The boat left shortly after I boarded it. Rows of warehouses could be seen on both sides of the river, with many newly-built flats between the warehouses, and high tide had washed the banks of the river with mud and litter.

I had wondered about the names of places like 'East India Docks' and 'West India Quay' before visiting East London, and now I was curious to see the offices and warehouses used by the Company when it ruled the Indian subcontinent. A few of its buildings in the City had disappeared. One day, while cycling towards East India Dock Road from the City, I found a building that was reminiscent of Lutyens' Delhi. The building seemed too quiet for any commercial activity to be taking place inside it. Perhaps it had been turned into residential flats, like other warehouses in the area.

Approaching the high-rise buildings around Canary Wharf by water, I couldn't associate the cityscape in front of me with London. It felt for a moment as if I were travelling in another country. I was baffled by the name 'Canary Wharf' until I learned that it was where tomatoes from the Canary Islands arrived in Britain.

The sight of neoclassical buildings heralded our destination before our boat moored at Greenwich Pier. There was a docked ship nearby, which I remembered seeing on my first visit, but I couldn't figure out why it was called 'Cutty Sark'. I found a guide in front of the ship who was leading a small walking group and reciting the Robert Burns poem, 'Tam-o-Shanter', in its entirety to his audience. He then told them that the name of the ship came from the shirt worn by a witch in the poem. The ship was built to sail swiftly across the oceans to bring a fresh crop of tea to Britain from China but was later used to bring wool from New Zealand.

I wanted to visit the Queen's House, designed by Inigo Jones. The house was built in Palladian style with colonnaded wings on both sides. There were some interesting paintings inside. One of them was by Canaletto, in which he had painted the Queen's House with a slanting roof instead of a flat one. I had been drawn to Greenwich again by Canaletto's paintings. On one of the walls was the portrait of Inigo Jones. It looked as if Rembrandt had grown a pointed beard in his self-portrait in order to resemble Jones.

After leaving the Queen's House, I walked towards the Painted Hall, used until recently as a dining hall by the Royal Naval College. I was surprised to learn that the hall was designed by Christopher Wren. It was astonishing how many monumental buildings Wren designed in his lifetime. The hall was painted by James Thornhill over a number of years, its main ceiling depicting the virtues of the monarchy. A mirror had been placed on a wheeled frame in the hall to make it easier for visitors to see the ceiling.

The hall was illuminated by an array of candelabras placed on dining tables. I wondered why the room wasn't filled with smoke until I realized that the candelabras were fitted with electric bulbs in the shape of candles. At the far end of the hall, a wreath of fresh flowers had been placed in memory of Admiral Lord Nelson. He was still being commemorated in the Painted Hall a couple of months after the 200th anniversary of his death.

Christopher Wren and his apprentice, Nicholas Hawksmoor, had designed the Royal Hospital in Greenwich for men who served in the Royal Navy and could not support themselves in old age. But it was deemed too grand to be an almshouse and was later adapted for use as the Royal Naval College. The splendid dining room of the College had been used by men trained to be masters of the sea when Britain was a major colonial power. In fact, it was the superiority of its naval forces that had resulted in the formation of an empire. The grand architecture of the seamen's town that was Greenwich bears witness to the past naval power of Britain.

I walked through a tunnelled passage from the Painted Hall to see the Chapel of St Peter and St Paul. Above the entrance of the Chapel was a biblical inscription, 'Blessed are the meek: for they shall inherit the earth'. It made me wonder when it was in the history of mankind that the meek had inherited the earth. Perhaps the Lord had made this promise to keep the meek resigned to their misery. Britain had subjugated the meek nations of the world by the might of its navy. I actually found a statue of Meekness made of artificial stone inside the Chapel. The interior of the Chapel was very colourful and I was captivated by the intricate patterns on its ceiling.

In need of refreshment before visiting the Royal Observatory, I found a coffee-shop inside one of the buildings at the bottom of the hill. It was crowded with visitors to Greenwich. Accordingly, there was a display of wooden models of various ships on one of its walls.

There were just a few people walking along the paths that traverse the hill but more were walking up and down the tree-lined path to the observatory. I hadn't been inside it on my previous visit to Greenwich. Standing on top of the hill, I found the landscape had changed since that first visit eleven years ago. I remembered tall chimneys rising from a brick building, but a large dome had appeared nearby in celebration of the millennium. One could see as far as Hampstead and Highgate in the green landscape painted by Johannes Vorsterman displayed in the Queen's House. However, I was distracted by the reflective exterior of the high-rise buildings around Canary Wharf, which were not too far from the hill. From Parliament Hill in Hampstead, I used to see the pyramid top of the Canary Wharf Tower emitting silver light, intermittently warning of some incoming danger.

The Royal Observatory was designed by Wren, who was an astronomer as well as an architect. The names of men who had served as Astronomers Royal were posted on a board inside the observatory. It was news to me that the English monarchy appointed a Royal Astronomer just as they chose a Poet Laureate who would occasionally compose a poem in their honour.

I was inside the observatory looking at the exhibits when a man appeared in the attire of a courtier and began to lecture. He explained how Greenwich was chosen as the Prime Meridian. It was in fact an American professor, he said, who proposed in 1870 that the Greenwich Meridian should be used as the basis of the world time-zone system. A few years later in 1884 the International Meridian Conference in Washington conferred the status of Prime Meridian on Greenwich, thanks to John Harrison's achievement in making an accurate clock for finding the longitude of ships at sea. Also, Britain was at the height of its imperial power at the end of the nineteenth century so it was unlikely that this distinction would have been conferred on Paris or Vienna.

As the Royal Observatory was currently undergoing refurbishment only a part of it was open to the public. The lecturer apologized for this and asked his audience to come back a few months later to see the remaining sections. He then asked if anybody had a question for him. An absent-minded Australian woman asked him if the Queen's House was in the Northern or the Southern Hemisphere. The guide was amused and replied "Ma'am, you are in the Northern Hemisphere until you fly back to Sydney."

The shop in the observatory was full of people buying souvenirs, and a perpetual photo-shoot taking place outside made it difficult to walk towards the gates without getting in the way of photographers.

I had spent some time in a covered market on my first visit to Greenwich, but I had only a vague recall of its location. I passed the buildings of Greenwich University towards the main road and then crossed over to a passage which, luckily, led to the market. A large group of Italian students browsed at the market stalls. During my earlier visit there, a shopkeeper told me that Italians were very fond of markets in London. I would have liked to say hello to him but the shop had a different owner now. Many of the shops there had changed hands. The stallholders were selling old compasses, maps and various nautical instruments. One was selling second-hand books. I browsed the stall in vain for something interesting but it mostly sold books of the coffee-table variety.

Greenwich Pier was only a short distance away from the market. I had found the entrance of a foot tunnel with a domed roof above it when I got off the boat in the morning. Now I wanted to cross it to see Greenwich from the north bank of the Thames, where Canaletto had set up his easel when he had painted the neoclassical buildings in the town. The river in his painting is busy with boats sailing up and down. However, it looked desolate now with no boats or barges crossing it.

I entered the rotunda to reach the foot tunnel under the Thames. The lift to the tunnel was broken so I had to climb down a spiral staircase to reach it. This tunnel appeared shallower than many underground stations in London. It was built like a suspension bridge made of ropes that dips in the middle. No one else was walking inside the tunnel. Perhaps people were frightened to cross it on their own or it was too long a walk for them. It was while crossing the tunnel by foot that I realized how far apart the banks of the Thames are near Greenwich. Looking across water sometimes creates an illusion that the other side is nearer than it actually is.

The lift on the other side was also out of order. Could the lifts have been put out of service purposely? But the stairs were wide and had low risers so it was easy to climb up.

Greenwich looked serene from this side of the river. There were a few benches along the riverbank for enjoying the view. I followed a sign to a train station called Island Gardens to get back to Tower Hill. The train passed through a landscape that was new to me. There were signboards everywhere for properties for sale, most of them newly built. This was obviously not meant to regenerate the area for many but to create wealth for a few.

I had taken a train in the wrong direction and had to get off to change lines in order to take the right train to Tower Hill. By the time I arrived, it was closing time at the Tower of London and many tourists were heading for the Underground. I was glad to cut through the City on my bicycle. City workers were leaving their offices in large numbers to go home. Someone living in the City once told me that its population was smaller than it was a few hundred years ago. St Paul's looked different after having its exterior cleaned. The cathedral was engulfed by more pedestrians in the evening than I had seen during the day. I cycled down Ludgate Hill to the less crowded Fleet Street.

The London I had heard about in my childhood in Kashmir was a city where people were compassionate, shopkeepers were honest and democracy was valued. Britain was the country of origin of the head teacher of a missionary school in Srinagar who was revered by everyone. One day I was browsing in the Oriental and India Office archives in the British Library when I came across a book in which this head teacher had some sordid things to say about the people in Kashmir who had held him in such high esteem. Then I met one or two people in London who had spent a few months in Kashmir. They had gone there with very little money but were befriended by local men who had taken care of them. I found them constantly worrying about the prospect of one of them ever coming to London to be their guest.

When I saw the Houses of Parliament for the first time, I was intrigued by its mock Gothic architecture. I sometimes crossed Westminster Bridge to go to the South Bank Centre. It pleased me to spot the odd parliamentarian cycling to the House of Commons. I was thrilled when I reached the voting age in Kashmir, but in London found to my dismay that only half of the electorate cast their votes in parliamentary elections. It seemed absurd that Britain was waging war in the 21st century on the pretext of bringing democracy to another country when only half of its own people wished to exercise their right to vote. I admit that I myself sided with those people in Britain who chose not to cast their votes. However, I was puzzled to find that one of the Houses of Parliament was undemocratic in a country which is regarded as the mother of parliamentary democracy in the world.

I didn't really know the meaning of colonialism and its aftermath until I came to Britain. I had mistakenly believed the British Empire to be benevolent and I couldn't see the point of wailing about colonialism half a century after its demise. I even found it disturbing in the beginning when an elderly Bengali man told me that he was justified in getting handouts in London because Britain had prospered from colonialism. But I began to understand the meaning of imperialism after living in London for a few years. As I came to discover the city, I realized the role imperialism had played in the making of the capital and how much of it was built at a time when Queen Victoria was proclaimed the Empress of India.

The British Empire had fostered the propagation of Anglicanism in various African and Asian countries under its rule. It had a proselytising effect on its subjects like other empires before it. I was surprised to find an abbey beside the Houses of Parliament, and in fact mistook it for a part of Parliament during my first few months in London. Then I gradually came to understand the old alliance whereby the monarch is regarded as guardian of the faith and Parliament is considered to be subservient to the Crown.

I also understood, as an outcome of the Empire, the dominance of one culture over many others in the world. The British Empire resulted in the spreading of the English language across the globe. It would be wrong to believe that English is more logical and easier to learn than other languages, yet it is chosen as the lingua franca in most countries around the world. Hence a cultural empire was established after the end of the political one. I once met someone in London who was teaching English in Brazil. She told me that she earned more there than she had earned in London and was able to send money to London to pay off her debts. I subsequently found many Brazilians working very hard in London for very little money in order to learn English.

I recently stood before a magistrate who stated, while leafing through my first book, that he had to ask me a question that was legally required. He then asked me if I spoke English. Whereas the magistrate no doubt thought that he was simply upholding the law, I felt humiliated. I didn't mind a tramp in London asking me such a question now and again, but I thought that an English magistrate would have been more considerate. When I saw the royal motto, 'Dieu et mon droit', mounted on the wall behind the magistrate, it occurred to me that it was perhaps his divine right to humiliate someone like me who was neither English nor British. My false idea of the benevolence of Britain as an imperial nation vanished when I heard debates in the House of Commons in which the elected members unashamedly asserted self-interest while discussing Britain's current role in world affairs.

I set out on this journey so that I could see some unfamiliar towns like Birmingham, Sheffield and Glasgow, which I otherwise had no excuse to visit, as well as those I wished to know better. When I mentioned my plans to visit these towns to a few people who knew me in London, they expressed doubts about how I was going to manage to travel the country. Perhaps they were aware of my meagre resources. But in the end it took strength of will for me to get out of London for a day or two. And yet I longed to be back in the town every night I spent away from it.

For many years, I had found London too full of distractions to undertake any writing. But eventually I felt the emptiness of living a solitary life at the edge of Hampstead Heath, and one day I met an author in my neighbourhood who told me that it is the indifference of Londoners that I might find useful as a writer. In fact, it was the bustle in the coffee-shops around the town which provided me with the solitude to concentrate on writing a book. I had spent many nights in the West End after finishing work during my first few years in London. But I reversed this habit by spending my days there and going to work in the evening outside Central London.

I had arrived in Britain with an American travel guide notion of it being the 'genuinely most civilized' country in the world. Then I discovered that Britain has one of the world's largest prison populations. How can a genuinely civilized country keep so many of its people behind bars? It was like catching a glimpse of the dark side of the moon. I had also mistakenly believed that if there was a socialist country anywhere in the world it was Britain. But I saw as much social inequality here as elsewhere. It is not my eye but my heart which has perhaps changed after living a circumscribed life in the country which once ruled the world.

October 2004 – December 2005

Acknowledgements

Andrew Stilwell, David & Jean Levy,
Patrick Walsh, Ruth Padel,
Mehmood Durrani, Dermot Torney,
Charles Beckett, Kate Griffin,
Leila Alhirsi, Tasaduq Hussein,
Martin Koerner, Imtiaz Khaja,
Sebastian Sardou, Robert Lambolle,
Stella Okoli, Jaleel Ahmed,
Bernadette, Ian, Roger Clinton-Smith